"Nate Adams has a wonderful ability to see humor in drab, ordinary moments, and to cut to the heart of the matter. Here's a wry, wise, biblical look at men's foibles, fears, uniqueness—and unlimited potential."

Harold Myra, President of
Christianity Today, Inc.

"*Separating the Men from the Boys* has a way of sneaking up on you. Nate Adams has written a useful, contemporary book that is aware of the tensions in modern manhood. This is not a scalding, 'ain't it awful,' book, but a positive reinforcement of the best in us. These are the issues that must be faced by all maturing men, yet they are faced in good humor, undergirded by solid biblical principles."

Jay Kesler, President of Taylor University.

"Just when you start bemoaning the day you became a man—with all the irritating hassles that come with being a responsible grownup—along comes Nate Adams to tell you it's still okay to have some little boy left in you. With humorous and genuine 'slingshot in the backpocket' guy stories, Adams tells us what it is about boyhood that we can take along with us as we metamorphize from exuberant boys to godly men."

Dave Branon, Managing Editor of
Sports Spectrum magazine

"Finally! A book for men written by someone who doesn't make us feel insecure or inadequate! There's spiritual depth and lots of solid encouragement here, all packaged in a humorous, conversational style that makes this book worth a second—and third—read. Well done, Nate!"

Harold B. Smith, author of
Hey Dad! Are We There Yet?

Nine Character Traits

Separating

the MEN from the BOYS

How Men Grow Up... and Why They Sometimes Don't

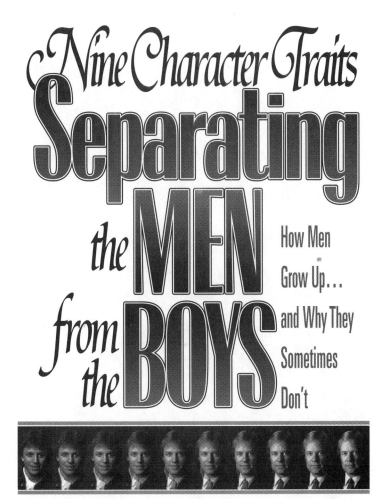

NATE ADAMS

BETHANY HOUSE PUBLISHERS

Minneapolis, MN 55438

All scripture quotations, unless indicated, are from the *Good News Bible,*
the Bible in Today's English Version. Copyright © American Bible
Society 1966, 1971, 1976.

Published by Bethany House Publishers
A Ministry of Bethany Fellowship, Inc.
11300 Hampshire Avenue South
Minneapolis, Minnesota 55438

Library of Congress Cataloging-in-Publication Data

Adams, Nate
    Nine character traits separating the men from the boys / Nate
Adams.
        p.   cm.

    1. Men—Religious life. 2. Maturation (Psychology)—Religious
aspects—Christianity.   I. Title.
BV4528.2.A33   1994
248.8'42—dc20   94–8449
ISBN 1–55661–458–6   CIP

To the significant men in my life—
Dad, my example
Roy, my encourager
Don, Scott, and Tim, my close friends

And the significant boys in my life—
Caleb, Noah, and Ethan, my three sons

With love for my wife, Beth, who married a less than perfect guy
And worship for the Lord Jesus, the perfect guy I want to be like

NATE ADAMS is Vice-President of Marketing at Christianity To-day, Inc. He has written twenty of the popular "Eutychus" col-umns for *Christianity Today*, and he has edited and written for the "For Men Only" section of *Marraige Partnership*. He has also writ-ten a fun-and-serious youth devotional book entitled, *Energizers, Light Devotions To Keep Your Faith Growing*. An ordained minister, he also serves the local church as an adult Sunday School teacher, deacon, worship leader, choir director, and guest speaker.

CONTENTS

Part 5: HUMILITY in Relationships

Part 6: FOCUS in Priorities

Part 7: PURITY in Motives

Part 8: DISCERNMENT in Values

Part 9: WISDOM in Perspective

INTRODUCTION

Men Will Be Boys

When I get home from work each day, my wife, Beth, and I go through a little ritual. Actually, it's only a ritual in the same sense that clubbing cavewomen over the head and dragging them off in courtship was a ritual. The cavewoman was sort of an unwilling participant, and in our ritual Beth probably characterizes herself the same way.

Beth usually sits on our bed so we can talk while I change into my jeans. As I'm walking around hanging things up and putting things away (like all well-trained husbands), I'll carefully look for an opportunity to nonchalantly walk within reach of her. Then I'll take the dirty socks that have been concealed in my hand, thrust them in her face, and revel in her cries of disgust. We've been married almost nine years now. I'd say we've been doing the sock thing for about eight and a half.

Of course, lest you think too critically of my sweet wife or how long it takes her to catch on to something, you should know Beth has learned to cover her face with her hand every time I come anywhere near her during the clothes-changing process. As long as I see she's "covering up," I won't force the sock ritual upon her. It's enough for me just to know she's thinking about it. And because she's learned to be aware of where my dirty socks are and put her guard up so reflexively, I only find an opening about once every two or three weeks.

But boy, when I do score, you should see the celebration. A few dance steps around the bedroom, a slam dunk of the socks into the clothes hamper (I'm still well-trained, in spite of my juvenile tendencies), and a hands-over-the-head taunt of my bested opponent that would outshine most end-zone celebrations in the NFL.

Why do I do stuff like that? Well, don't think that Beth didn't ask that same question the first year or two we were married. But I couldn't really give her a satisfactory answer, except that I was exempt from prosecution under the "boys will be boys" statute that has governed male behavior and misbehavior for years.

Even though I'm a grown man, a husband, a father, a church leader, a professional—there's still a lot of boy in me. You'd think that the responsibility of parenting our three young children would have driven away most of my male adolescence. But do you know what I sent my younger sister in the mail a few weeks after each of our kids was born? Actually, she didn't know what the first one was herself, even after she opened the little box and held it in her hand. Then when she called me and found out it was the dried-up umbilical cord that had finally fallen out of her new nephew's navel— well, I could still hear the shriek long after she dropped the phone. In fact, I think I could hear it after she hung up the phone.

I read a magazine article recently which made the statement, "The American male doesn't mature until he has exhausted all possibilities." Bingo! Boyish behavior is a lifelong reality for us guys. We can't help it. We don't want to help it. And I would contend that in many ways, we're not supposed to. That same playful energy, that boyish charm, that frog-in-the-pocket adventure that we bring to life are at least part of what make us attractive to the girls and women who choose to love us.

So let's start with that assumption. The boy in us is here to stay. And let's take it one step further. The boy in us can be a very positive part of who we are. In his childlikeness he can be playful and fun-loving and carefree. He can be trusting and teachable and honest. The boy in us is the part still unsullied by the cares of the world, untainted by contagious prejudices, unafraid of the obstacles that may lie before him. As guys, the boy in us can be one of the best things we have going.

At that time the disciples came to Jesus, asking, "Who is the greatest in the Kingdom of heaven?" So Jesus called a child, had him stand in front of them, and said, "I assure you that unless you change and become like children, you will never enter the Kingdom of heaven." (Matthew 18:1–3)

Boys Will Be Men, Too

Beth and I have three boys. Caleb is five, Noah is four, and Ethan just joined us a few weeks ago. I sometimes feel immersed in a pool of boyishness. And when you add my own boyishness to the pool, well, I think it can sometimes make Beth feel she's been immersed too long and needs to come up for air.

Especially as they get older, my three sons (da da da daaaaaaa . . . da da da daaaaaaaa . . . hum to the tune of the *My Three Sons* theme song) remind me more and more of what it was like to be a boy, especially one growing up with brothers. I thought my brothers and I were the only ones who cared so passionately about who got to sit where in the car. But even when Caleb and Noah were both still in car seats they were having the same conflict.

One day Noah decided for some reason that he wanted to sit in Caleb's car seat. Attempts to reason with him proved futile. He couldn't even express to us why he wanted the other seat so desperately. Finally, Beth appealed to him with the simple truth: "But, Noah, that's your brother's car seat!"

Neither of us was ready for his mercenary retort, "Then I don't want him to be my brother!"

Beth looked at me as if to say that such statements of principle and consequence are to be handled by fathers. I cleared my throat to make room for the profundity that would emerge, and then decided to use every dad's secret weapon—guilt.

"Why, Noah," I began with a serious tone, "are you saying you'd rather have Caleb's car seat than to have him as a brother?" Unfortunately, to Noah it may have sounded more like a legitimate offer than the hypothetical anathema I had intended it to be.

"Okay," he replied sweetly, and hopped up into Caleb's car seat as if he expected me to go draw up the necessary papers.

But if we were caught off guard by Noah's boyish declaration, we were even less ready for Caleb's response. He looked at Beth—probably feeling that I had not done the best possible job of negotiating his position in the matter—and said, "Mommy, I don't want to stop being Noah's brother. He can sit in my car seat."

You see, boys are just as likely to surprise you with their displays of manhood as men are with their displays of boyhood. Caleb had just demonstrated his willingness to put relationship before possession and position. I know a lot of full-grown men, myself included, who often don't demonstrate that kind of maturity.

So let's add another assumption to our list. Guys are intended to grow up. The man in us exists at all ages, just like the boy in us, and he too can be a very positive part of who we are. In his manhood he can abandon the childish ways that tend to be self-oriented and hurtful to others. He can be thoughtful and responsible and sacrificial. The man in us is the part who has learned to deny or postpone his own desires, who has learned patience by virtue of his experience, who has learned the value of taking the long view. As guys, the man in us can also be one of the best things we have going.

> When I was a child, my speech, feelings, and thinking were all those of a child; now that I am a man, I have no more use for childish ways. (1 Corinthians 13:11)

The Friendly Tug-of-War

On the outside chance that you're reading this introduction in order to discover the book's premise, let me go ahead and give it to you. Of course, if it's the boy in you who reads books, you probably skipped this part altogether and dived right into Chapter 1—that's what I usually do. If it's the man in you who reads books, you're probably getting impatient with me right now because you want to nail down the premise, set the context, and get on with the serious task of reading.

Okay, here it is. As guys, the development of our maturity and character could be described as a tug-of-war between the boy in us and the man in us. It's mostly a friendly tug-of-war, with the boy and the man pretty evenly matched. Sometimes the man gives ground to the youth and strength of the boy, and at other times the boy gives ground to the knowledge and experience of the man.

Why won't the man let go? He knows we're designed to grow up. His role in the development of our character is to see that we're taking life seriously and responsibly. Why won't the boy let go? He knows that in many ways we're better off staying childlike as we grow. His role is to see that we're keeping our life simple, trusting, and passionate.

Generally speaking, the boy in us is more true to our heart, while the man in us is more true to our head. The man in us tells the boy in us to "grow up." The boy in us tells the man in us to "lighten up." It's not unlike the conversation fathers and teenage sons have almost every day.

This friendly tug is not without its villains, however. Occasionally, either the boy or the man in us will lose so much ground that one will be dragged into the mud pit that so often separates even friendly tugs-of-war. When the healthy tension between the boy in us and the man in us is removed, one of two new characters may surface. The "brat" in us is the boy in excess, without the balancing influence of the man. The "jerk" in us is the man in excess, without the balancing influence of the boy. As we'll see during the following pages, these two aren't guys we want ruling our character or our lives.

You see, the differences between the boy and the brat and between the man and the jerk are like the difference between night and day. Sure, a *maturing, childlike* guy may occasionally make those around him roll their eyes in disbelief as he grudgingly holds on to his favorite hobby or goofy sense of humor. But an *immature, childish* guy is more likely to be a source of hurt or a target of nagging to those around him—those who wish he'd lead his family, keep his job, stop hurting his children, or just plain grow up and think of someone besides himself.

The Point of Separation

When my brother and I were teenagers, there was plenty of tension between us, just as there is between the boy in us and the man in us. One evening at supper, the tension between us over a series of disagreements had just about snapped our rope. When he put a large portion of mashed potatoes on his plate, I may have exaggerated my characterization of his appetite. As he returned a bitter reply, we both came to our feet.

Before my parents knew what was happening, we were locked together in a rock-em-sock-em punch fest that knocked over our chairs and sent us tumbling into the next room and over the couch. My mom was crying, "Tom, they're going to kill each other! Separate them! SEPARATE THEM!"

At that point, my father decided to put down his fork. My brother and I were already about punched out, yet unwilling to be the first to call it quits. I remember wondering where our normal parental intervention had gone. My dad just stood and watched us fight. He made sure we weren't breaking anything, but then merely let us wear ourselves out. Eventually we gave in to mutual exhaustion, and just lay there heaving heavy breaths. It was the last physical fight we ever had.

I think Dad chose not to separate us that day because he realized that at some point people have to do their own separating and work out their own balances of power. That's true of this book, too. In these few pages we can't unravel all the deep psychological and spiritual factors that make us who we are. Each of us has to work out our own internal balance of power between the boy in us and the man in us. But we can start by separating those two key characters in our personality in order to understand their different influences on us. And we can look at nine different "arenas" of life where a balance between the boy and the man can produce very positive character traits. In doing so, perhaps we can better understand how we guys mature, and why we sometimes don't.

I've chosen to tell a lot of stories and personal experiences in these pages because lots of times I think they speak better for themselves than any principles or platitudes I could articulate. They're true, everyday-type stories, because that's where our characters are really displayed—in true, everyday circumstances, not just the times when we're willing to show them. The stories are intended to make us think about real life the way it happens. But more than that, I hope they'll help make clear the character traits that are worth developing to give our lives success from God's perspective.

A guy's character is not simple or homogenous. There are many different character qualities that demonstrate themselves in many different arenas of life. Some of those arenas are deep within us, and our maturity or immaturity there is often detectable only by those closest to us. Other arenas are so public and visible that almost everyone around us is invited to a view of our inner character. And none of those is more apparent to others than the arena of our work and our play.

SEPARATING THE MEN

Chapter / Topic	The Boy in Us...	The Brat in Us...	The Man in Us...
1. Work and Play	...works and plays with enthusiasm	...is always bored	...works and plays with diligence
2. Decisions	...makes decisions based on passion	...is always emotional	...makes decisions based on principle
3. Discipline	...brings motivation to discipline	...is always reckless	...brings caution to discipline
4. Communication	...communicates with truthfulness	...is always judgmental	...communicates with tact
5. Relationships	...takes pleasure from others in relationships	...is always self-gratifying	...takes responsibility for others in relationships
6. Priorities	...sets priorities out of a determination to do one thing	...is always preoccupied	...sets priorities out of a desire to do many things
7. Motives	...has motives that listen to inside voices	...is always self-serving	...has motives that listen to outside voices
8. Values	...values the immediate	...is always nearsighted	...values the eventual
9. Perspective	...has a perspective that perceives our significance	...is always conceited	...has a perspective that perceives our insignificance

FROM THE BOYS

The Jerk in Us...	Balanced Character Trait
...is always task-oriented	CREATIVITY "Finding the fun in what needs to be done"
...is always rigid	RESPONSIBILITY "Acting with might when you know what is right"
...is always fearful	PATIENCE "Moving toward goals while balancing roles"
...is always cowardly	LOVE "Saying what's true with encouragement too"
...is always authoritative	HUMILITY "Seeking good for another without trying to smother"
...is always distracted	PURPOSEFULNESS "Staying on track without breaking your back"
...is always man-pleasing	PURITY "Following dreams without plotting schemes"
...is always farsighted	DISCERNMENT "Embracing today in an eternal way"
...is always feeling worthless	WISDOM "Understanding your place in the context of grace"

Character Trait #1
Creativity
in Work and Play

...means finding the FUN in what needs to be DONE

LABOR DAY AND GUYS AT PLAY

"Fridays Only Shalt Thou Labor . . . Okay, Honey?"

A few years ago my wife, Beth, celebrated Labor Day weekend in the most appropriate of ways. She went into labor. Our first child was born on a Friday night, leaving the holiday weekend ahead of us to start making the transition from a twosome to a threesome.

I remember thinking that even though Caleb's arrival was a week past his "due date" (a term I've since come to understand as mythological), the timing of his birth was actually quite convenient. The Friday night arrival meant I could hang around the hospital most of the weekend, friends and family could be more free to come and visit us, and most importantly—we could be home and settled before I had to miss a day of work.

That's the way the pioneers used to do it, right? Husband and expectant wife would work side by side in the fields right up to the last minute. When labor came they'd spread some blankets a respectable distance from the field, birth the baby, give the wife the afternoon off, and send the husband back to the plow.

Of course now we have it pretty soft compared to the pioneers. Five-day workweeks, more flexible schedules, and frequent holidays mean we spoiled twentieth-century men can even take a couple of days off from work to be sensitive bedside partners. But then back to the plow, right?

When Caleb was born and I realized the efficiency of this strategy, I decided then and there that any future children of ours should be born on the Friday of a holiday weekend. I jotted a note to discuss it with Beth and the doctor sometime when they weren't so busy.

Serious Play

Caleb's birth happened back in the days when insurance companies didn't categorize baby-delivering along with things like wart removal as deserving only an overnight hospital stay. We were told Beth could plan on spending three nights in the hospital and probably go home the following Monday. This brought up the question of whether we should still host the thirty people we had invited to our house for a Labor Day cookout.

I know what you're thinking. What kind of insane people would have thirty people coming to their house right after their baby is born? Well, remember, Caleb was our first child. We just didn't know any better. Plus, he was a week overdue—we thought it would be a full ten days after his arrival that we'd have a house full of company. The main reason I wanted to press on with our plans, however, was that Labor Day at our house had become a tradition that extended far beyond lawn chairs and grilled burgers, especially for the guys in our group. Labor Day at our house meant—killer volleyball.

Preparation for killer volleyball is a serious and meticulous chore. Two days ahead of time I go out in our backyard and note the exact sun and shadow angles. Then I use a measuring tape to pace off precise dimensions for the court. Revving up the lawn mower, I mow the remainder of the yard, leaving the tall grass as a well-marked, high-traction playing surface, complete with four bright orange cones marking each corner. A regulation ball, an official net, and sturdy poles staked to perfection complete an outdoor court that would make any head groundskeeper proud.

New baby or not, how could we cancel killer volleyball? I figured Beth and Caleb would be in the hospital until Monday evening anyway, and they could probably use one last restful day of hand-and-foot service before coming home to reality. Beth reluctantly bought in to my logic (she seems to reason better when heavily sedated), and we decided I would proceed with killer volleyball—and the cookout—as planned.

In my mind, this first birth couldn't have gone any better. Beth had come through okay, the baby was healthy, I wasn't going to miss much work, and Labor Day's killer volleyball could go on unhindered. It wasn't until the very end of the weekend that I apparently blew it. Tied 7–7 in our best of 15 series, we were just underway in the championship game at dusk when the phone rang. It was Beth.

"Guess what?" she bubbled. "The doctor has released us. We're ready to come home!"

Now I know the right answer was for me to say I'd drop everything and be right there. I know the game and the party could have gone on or wound down without me. I know this was my only begotten son. But my beloved's voice on the phone somehow couldn't overcome the intoxicating view of my manicured center court and the impatient looks of my teammates. Before I knew it, the words were out. And those same words that had brought the wrath of my mother for so many years now brought the wrath of my new son's mother.

"Just let me finish this one game."

All Work and All Play Make Johnny a Classic Guy

That Labor Day weekend I proved to myself, and to my wife, the amazing gravitational pull both work and play have in a guy's life. My wife was lying exhausted in a hospital bed and I was glad it was on a Friday so I wouldn't miss work. My son had just come into the world and I wanted to finish game 15 before bringing him home.

Work and play may sound like opposites, but they're remarkably similar and strong factors in a guy's life. Consider this statement of philosophy from the Discovery Toys catalog: "We believe that play is a child's work . . . children play to learn, to grow, and to experience the world around them." I think they've hit the plastic nail right on the head. Play is a boy's work. Work, in many ways, is a man's play. Both our work and our play are challenges we pour ourselves into because they help us define who we are and measure what we can do.

As a result, a guy's work and play are usually the most public and visible arenas in which he demonstrates his maturity and character. If you'll pay attention, I'll show you more of myself in a half-hour tennis match than you'd learn in a two-hour interview. Work alongside me for a day and you'll have an even better inside look at what makes me tick.

We spend a lot of our time and concentrated effort at work, and it's usually pretty important to us. Work is where we live most of our waking hours. In most cases, it's where we get a strong sense of purpose, of productivity, of usefulness, of value. It's how we provide for those we love. It's how we demonstrate our skill. It's how we pay our bills.

The quality and quantity of our work can also determine how much freedom we have to play. In fact, it's probably that word *freedom* that best explains why a guy's play is so important to him, too. The boy in me remembers when I could walk out into a summer day and do almost anything I wanted. Ride my bike, play baseball, watch TV, go to a friend's house—sure there were limitations and boundaries on my freedom then, but I don't really remember them. I just remember each day for what it was—the pursuit of fun.

The Fun Factor

Guys run on fun. That's why you can never go through a little boy's closet and throw away his old toys. Everything you find reminds him of some fun he once had, and he doesn't want to let go of it. The conversation usually goes something like this:

"Hey, remember this old toy? Why don't we give this away to the church nursery?"

"No."

"Why not?"

"I want it."

"Want it? You haven't played with this in three years. It's been here on the top shelf of your closet gathering dust. You've got all kinds of new toys that are tons better than this. And you're too big to play with this anyway. Let's get rid of it."

"I want it."

The same scenario happens when you try to clean out a grown-up boy's closet. Take, for instance, the wife trying to throw out the husband's favorite sweater—the one he scored two touchdowns in when he and the guys used to play football:

"Hey, remember this? Why don't we give this away to the Salvation Army?"

"No."

"Why not?"

"I want it."

"Want it? You haven't worn it in three years. It's been buried in your drawer taking up valuable space. You've got all kinds of new sweaters that aren't ten years out of style. And it's too tight on you anyway. Let's get rid of it."

"I want it."

Yes, guys are definitely into fun. If I had a dollar for every time my sons asked me, "Dad, can't you think of anything FUN to do?"—well, I could put them on the next plane to Disney World and solve both our problems.

Yet this boyish love of fun can be a very good thing. A guy's desire to have fun can give him almost boundless energy. When play is fun, we approach it with infectious enthusiasm. When work is fun, we're more diligent and accomplish more. We've all seen professional athletes who clearly view their sport as a job, or more to the point, a business. Whatever admiration we might have for their skill, they're not as enjoyable to watch.

Then there's the guy who loves the game. Even if he makes millions, you get the idea he'd play for nothing. It doesn't matter whether he's having a good day or not. He plays hard. He laughs at himself. He dives. He gets dirty. He jumps right up when he falls down. He goes crazy when his team scores. He winks at the camera. At the same time he's enthusiastic in his play, he's also diligent in his work.

I'm not a professional athlete, but I too enjoy my day the most when I do the equivalent of those things. I arrange my desk and its contents just like I used to arrange my treasure box full of baseball cards and favorite rocks. I drink as much Coca-Cola as I want to, supplemented with candy from the office vending machine, and no one scolds me. I often play ball over my lunch hour. I "play" my competitors with the same shrewd methods that used to win Monopoly games. I call my co-workers my "team." I indulge in an occasional practical joke. I go to more birthday parties at the office than I ever did as I child. I make sure my computer has lots of fun loaded into it.

You can lock me in an office and tell me I'm a grown-up. You can remind me I'm a husband, and a father, and an educated professional. But I still run best on fun. And I'm at my best when I find a way to bring boyish enthusiasm to my play, and my work.

"CAN I PLAY TOO? CAN I PLAY TOO?"

The boy in us works and plays with enthusiasm

I was leading a small group discussion one time that had turned lively, humorous, and fun. Everyone was actively engaged in the topic, time was flying by, and we were all having a genuinely good time. Then with great enthusiasm, one young lady interjected a comment that stopped the lively banter cold in its tracks. I don't remember exactly what she said, because even at the time I had no idea how it pertained to what we were talking about.

Because I was the leader, and because you could almost see the skid marks where the discussion had screeched to a halt, I felt I had to try and build a bridge back to the original discussion from her apparently random comment. It was a big gulf to span.

"Tell me a little more of what you mean by that . . . " I ventured tentatively, hoping she'd somehow be able to help me see her point without being too awfully embarrassed. She wasn't embarrassed at all.

"Oh, I don't know how it fits in," she giggled. "I just wanted to participate!"

The group laughed with her, and we all jumped quickly back into the topic. No one thought any less of our friend or her conversational speed bump because we all knew what had happened. The fun atmosphere and compelling discussion had brought out that contagious quality of enthusiasm in all of us, and one of us had simply overdosed a little.

Wanting to participate just for the fun of it isn't a bad description of enthusiasm. People love being around a guy who's enthusiastic because he's so anxious to dig in and go at it. The enthusiastic person is the one who brings fun to whatever task is at hand.

When I bring boyish enthusiasm to my work, I find my co-workers will do almost anything I ask. Even if the project is difficult or unpleasant, it's as if they know one person's energy and upbeat attitude is the main thing needed to get the whole group through it. Just as one player's outstanding effort can lift the team and swing the entire momentum of a game, so my optimistic energy can give life and motivation to those around me.

Clothes Monster

My sons used to hate getting ready for bed. When bedtime came, we would gingerly announce that maybe it was time to start thinking about what incredibly fun thing they might like to do for just a few minutes before we started getting ready for . . . but we never made it to the word "bed" without weeping, wailing, whining, and impassioned pleas for amnesty. No matter how we tried to softpeddle it or how firm and stern we got about it, bedtime was always a nightly trauma. But that was before the Clothes Monster came to live at our house.

I don't remember planning the Clothes Monster or giving much thought to his creation. I just remember he came on a night when I felt playful and enthusiastic. When we announced bedtime to the boys, their reflex whines were immediately drowned out by my ferocious, ten-second roar. It startled everyone, including my wife, who probably thought my parental mind had finally snapped and had always believed she'd be the first to go. When they all realized that the roar came from me, they looked a little relieved and a little more scared at the same time. Dad only roars on special occasions.

The Clothes Monster then attacked the boys, tickling them, wrestling with them, "gobbling" at them, until their whines were long lost in giggles and squeals of laughter. In the process, of course, each article of clothing was removed and "gobbled up" (except my younger son's diaper—the Clothes Monster does have certain dietary standards). Bedtime was transformed from drudgery and the cessation of play into the nightly arrival of a new playmate, one whose very spirit was merely Dad's boyish enthusiasm.

There are lots of unpleasant tasks and difficult circumstances that come with family life, and life in general. But when the husband, father, or even the son looks those things in the face and smiles, when he communicates a "we can do it—and it will be FUN" attitude, he empowers everyone else with his enthusiasm.

It's the enthusiastic boy in us who helps us approach our work and our play with a sense of optimism and energy. I don't normally think of mowing the lawn as enjoyable, but when I'm mowing the lawn into a volleyball court I've found some fun to draw me into enjoying the task. I don't enjoy cleaning the gutters, but when the whole family puts up Christmas lights at the same time the task takes on a whole new atmosphere.

"I'm bored!" is something the boy in us says a lot. But what he's really saying is that he needs something to pour himself into, something about which he can be enthusiastic. He's looking for some fun, and if he can find it he'll bring great determination and energy to anything you put in front of him.

The Bored Brat in Us

Of course, boyish enthusiasm has a sort of dark side—a bratty side. It's the part of us that basically says, "If it's not fun, I'm not going to do it!" It's the brat in us who takes my boyish desire for fun and drives it to excess. Boys are cute. Brats are not. Boys are looking to create fun. Brats expect others to deliver fun to them on a silver platter. Instead of helping make me a motivating leader, the brat in me can make me an apathetic, reluctant follower. Instead of being a creator of fun and enthusiasm, he can make me look to others for entertainment or to make my life more enjoyable.

As husbands and fathers, brats are the ones who expect their family to wait on them. As friends, they're the ones who only give when there's something to get. As employees, they're the ones who never feel fairly treated or adequately rewarded. As bosses, they demand unchallenged authority. As basketball players, they're ball hogs. As sons, they expect lifelong handouts from Mom and Dad. Talking about brats as "them" is kind of cathartic, because we've all been annoyed by immature, self-serving people such as these. It's a little harder to admit that as a husband, father, friend, employee, boss, basketball player, or son we can sometimes "tilt" over into brattiness ourselves.

I remember grade school recesses when our principal (sort of a boyish enthusiast himself) would come out and quarterback both sides of our fifth-grade football games. In these fifteen-minute, all-out-effort contests, nobody wanted to be a blocker. Everyone wanted to go out for "the bomb."

Fortunately, no one on the defense wanted to rush the quarterback either. So every series, for four downs in a row, we'd line up 25 across in man-to-man coverage. Then the 25 receivers, dogged by 25 would-be interceptors, would take off in something resembling the invasion of Normandy. Principal Joe would rear back on one leg and heave a fifty-yard rainbow pass that sometimes was caught, and sometimes wasn't. Either way, there was always a large pile of fifth graders somewhere near the ball. We each had a one out of twenty-five chance of being thrown the ball, and considerably lesser odds of catching it. But we'd rather play those odds than play the trenches at the boring line of scrimmage. I found it paid to be a patient fifth grader during those games, because usually about halfway through recess, the ten or twelve guys who hadn't caught a bomb yet would get bored and go do something else.

The brat in us is like that. He likes the idea of catching the bomb, of having the fun, of soaking up the glory. But he never blocks. He never rushes the quarterback. Those things are drudgery, and drudgery is boring. The brat in us doesn't like to be bored. But somehow he can spend an amazing amount of our life in that very condition, because he expects others to set him free from his boredom, rather than walking out of it under his own power—the power of boyish enthusiasm.

Balancing the Boy

At his best, the boy in us looks for the "bright side" of things. He wants to enjoy both his play and his work, so he looks for ways to make them fun. When he succeeds, nothing can discourage him and everyone wants to follow him.

At his worst, the brat in us can make us addicted to fun and destined to boredom. He sees his work and his play through cynical eyes, and blames others for not making them more enjoyable for him. He refuses to take responsibility for his attitude, so he can never work his way out of his apathetic slouch. That's why a guy's boyish enthusiasm has to be balanced with diligence, and diligence is the contribution of the man in us.

"LET'S GET BUSY!"

The man in us works and plays with diligence

Fortunately, the "boy" in us has tugging against him the "man" in us, and this tension helps keep us from lapsing into the potential "brat" in us too often. While the boy in us loves fun and helps create a character of enthusiasm, the man in us has a slightly different agenda. He loves accomplishment and helps create a character of diligence.

The man in us loves to get things done. They may or may not be significant, profitable, or universally noble things, but they are the things he's deemed as important, and he very much wants to check them off his list.

A lot of people I've talked to find that this quality of diligence also has a slightly mutant strain found mostly in older fathers and fathers-in-law. Personally, I think they're just regular, diligent guys whose mutant condition you only encounter in awkward or unusual places—like your own home.

I've rarely heard of a father who can spend more than one night at his kids' house without going a little stir crazy. That's when his normally productive diligence can go a little haywire. Separated from his own list of things he needs to be doing, he's forced to share yours, or more likely, to re-create his list in your life. Before you know it, he's poking around in your tools, checking the air pressure in your tires, re-caulking your bathtub, and offering to fix noises you'd never noticed until he started tinkering with your home.

Of course, if he's not a particularly handy father or father-in-law, he may leave your stuff alone. Instead, he gets antsy to go places or do things that either contribute to his own "to do" list, or at least keep his mind off it. In other words, he needs to be busy.

31

If you deny him the diligent distraction of doing your chores or occupying your time, you're likely to find him parked sullenly in front of your TV with your remote control, a privilege you rarely share even with your wife. There he'll stay for the entire visit, a visit he keeps insisting to your mother or mother-in-law should end tomorrow.

The ironic thing is that grown sons and sons-in-law display the same fidgety behavior when the tables are turned. Personally, I never leave our house on vacation, or even to visit family, without packing my briefcase, planning calendar, laptop computer, and half a dozen books. The diligent man in me thrives on his pet list of productive things to do, and he can't leave home without it.

Congratulations, Grandpa, It's a Broken Appliance!

My wife's parents live about six hours away, and we don't get to see them as often as we'd like. Because of the long drive, we make the trip to their house more often than they can come to ours. Shortly after our first child was born (Labor Day weekend, remember?) we spoke to Beth's folks on the phone and suggested it might be nice if they could come to our house for the next visit. Beth's dad went into his usual litany bemoaning how far away we live, how hard the drive is, and how many things he had to do at home. Beth and I had already decided that my non-handiness was a much better lure for him than his only grandson.

"Gee, that's too bad, Dad," I remember Beth saying to him on the phone. "We just had to buy this new garbage disposal, and we're going to have to pay $85 to have it installed. We were wondering if that was something you knew anything about. . . ?"

"Eighty-five dollars!" he exclaimed. (When dealing with a depression-era father-in-law, there's nothing more powerful than threatening to pay a hefty price for a job you can theoretically do yourself.) "I can probably be there in a couple of days if you need me."

"Okay, Dad. Oh, by the way, bring Mom with you. She might want to see the new baby while you work on the disposal."

Yes, the diligent man in us thrives on having something to do. He loves being useful. He loves measurable progress. He loves working hard to save or make a buck. He's frugal. He's resourceful. He's persistent. Instead of counting sheep at night he counts projects being crossed off his "to do" list.

The diligent man in us brings an incredible work ethic to everything we do. He's the part of us that we want on our football team when we need an offensive lineman. He's the part of us we want working on a tedious project that has to be done right. He's the part of us who stays late and helps clean up, long after the enthusiastic party animals have gone home. Even when the job gets dirty or the hours get long, the diligent man in us keeps his focus and meets his deadlines.

As much as the enthusiastic boy in us runs on fun, the diligent man in us runs on productivity. In fact, to him, productivity is fun. While that may seem a little demented to those who don't understand, it's the love of productivity that enables us to undertake big projects, solve difficult problems, and survive catastrophic setbacks. The boy in us might encounter those things and turn away—better to start over on something new and fun than get dragged into such depressing activity. But the man in us uses his diligence to break down projects, problems, and setbacks into their manageable, solvable pieces. Then he rolls up his sleeves and stays after his plan until each piece is in its place, and each problem is conquered. Then he checks them off his list, and smiles.

The Task-Oriented Jerk in Us

Like enthusiasm, diligence can be taken to an extreme, especially when the man in us gets so consumed with the task that we lose consideration for the people involved. Then the man in us can become a "jerk" just as quickly as the boy in us can become a brat. If you think about it, some of the most monstrous jerks of history have been those so consumed with a warped mission, cause, or task that they shamelessly sacrificed their enemies and often their own people to accomplish it.

The jerk in us often grows out of good intentions. Something needs to be done or saved or written or managed or solved—and we seem to be the only one willing or able to do it. A sense of responsibility overtakes us and the challenges of the task pump our adrenalin. Crisis management kicks in and the consequences to people are deemed secondary. If they're not part of the solution, they're part of the problem. We don't have time to coddle or consult—there's a job to be done! Before we know it, the job has gotten out of control and people have been hurt. Unfortunately, the jerk in us doesn't usually care.

When I was a teenager, I was sometimes given the task of baby-sitting my younger brother and sister. They say that power corrupts, and power over younger siblings corrupts absolutely. Whenever Carey and Alita would get into trouble or disobey me, I'd punish them by making them clean various parts of the house. The bathrooms, of course, were always top on the list.

One night my parents came home to an exhausted little boy and girl with the cleanest fingernails you'd ever want to see. Mom asked how things had gone, and my little brother looked up through a tired, pine-scented scowl.

"You know, Mom," he said, "if anything ever happened to you and Dad and this guy took over for good, in a week the house would be spotless, and we'd both be dead."

Diligence, taken to an extreme, can create a jerk in us who refuses to admit there's time for play. He doesn't tolerate chitchat in the office. There's no room for goofing around at his dinner table. Fun and recreation are frivolous—there's a job to be done. And when this jerk is driving the car on vacation, pity the family member who needs to make a potty stop.

To the jerk in us, work is work and play is work. You never play a game just for the fun of it. You keep score. You compete and compare. There are always winners and losers, because how else can you measure your progress except by outdistancing others? It's often necessary to compromise the ideal in order to get the job done. Sometimes you even end up compromising what's right.

A friend of mine talks with teary eyes about the first time his one-year-old son called his name. My friend had been traveling a lot with his job, and was often gone days at a time during his son's first year. Coming home from one of those long business trips, he walked into the house, dropped to his knees, and held his arms open for his one-year-old.

"Honey, who's home?" his wife asked the baby boy.

Pointing to his dad, the one-year-old smiled and replied, "Bye-bye!"

It was then my friend realized that his son was referring to him. His little boy had learned to say his name from the many times Mommy had said, "Tell Daddy bye-bye."

That was the day my friend committed to finding a way to travel less, or finding a new job. His diligent work had gone too far.

Balancing the Man

The diligent man in us recognizes what needs doing and pursues it tenaciously. He's a workhorse who knows how to get the job done and is willing to make the necessary sacrifices. The diligent man in us can cope with things where the enthusiastic boy in us struggles, like losing at play or hardship at work. He can tolerate a thankless assignment because he's fueled more by tasks than people and more by productivity than fun.

But there's an important line between being task-oriented and being a taskmaster. When we let the diligent man in us dominate our work and play, we take both just a little too seriously. That's why we need a balance between the enthusiastic boy in us and the diligent man in us. To bring that balance, to find the fun in what needs to be done, requires the character trait of creativity.

FINDING THE FUN

In What Needs to Be Done

CREATIVITY in Work and Play:
Enthusiasm and Diligence in the Balance

What happens when the fun-loving, enthusiastic boy in me runs into the accomplishment-loving, diligent man in me? Or even scarier, what happens when the bored brat collides with the task-oriented jerk?

Picture a cool autumn Saturday morning. Dad, who has worked hard all week at a desk job, is girding up his loins to do the manly fall thing—leaf management. Unsuspecting son has just rolled out of bed, finished his breakfast, watched his cartoons, and is looking for some action.

"I'm bored!" he blunders.

Dad's eyes light up.

"Bored? BORED?" You'd think from Dad's tone that he's just been called a nasty name and challenged to a duel. Son realizes his mistake and, in a panic, tries to slither off to his room. It's too late.

"We wouldn't want you to be bored on a beautiful FALL day like today! Here, son, grab a rake and let me teach you the fine points of leaf management."

The boy is wanting to have some fun, to stir up some enthusiasm, to maybe get his dad to play something with him. The man is wanting to accomplish something, to lend diligence to a task that perhaps will show more productivity than anything he was able to get done at work all week. If they're not careful, they'll ruin each other's objectives as well as each other's Saturday, and both be miserable as a result. Dad's ability to accomplish will be dragged down by his son's pouty foot-dragging. The son's plea for play will also be cruelly rewarded. Hoping to toss the football around or go to a friend's house, he'll instead trade a moment of boredom for a morning of boredom at hard labor.

It's this kind of tug between man and boy that goes on continually within each one of us as we seek to balance fun with accomplishment. "Balancing" is really the key, and in the arena of work and play the mature balance between enthusiasm and diligence is found in a perhaps less-than-obvious character trait—creativity.

Unless you're God and can make something out of nothing, creativity can be humanly defined as transforming the ordinary into the original. It's putting things together—sometimes they're very different things, sometimes they're being put together for the first time—with imagination and skill to produce newness.

A guy who's striving for maturity in his character brings creativity to his work and his play. He holds on to his boyish enthusiasm, encouraging and motivating others. At the same time, he's diligent, working hard and playing hard, not just at the things he enjoys but at the things that are important. A creative guy finds the fun in what needs to be done.

"Tinkle Target" Creativity

A couple of years ago, I went through my first experience in potty training. (Actually it was my son's first experience. My own came much earlier in life, but I don't remember anything about it and tend not to trust my parents' jaded and selective accounts.) Our oldest two boys, Caleb and Noah, are only nineteen months apart, so they were kind of on the front end and the back end (if you'll pardon the expression) of potty training at the same time.

Fortunately, Beth got to deal with a lot more of this exciting phenomenon than I did. But even for me it seemed as if half my waking hours during those weeks were spent in the bathroom—encouraging, scolding, bribing, mopping, or just sighing with forced patience as I repeatedly saw the most sheepish smiles ever caused by non-performance.

You may not realize it, but potty training has been known to significantly improve adult literacy among parents of young children. That's because we pitiable parents are reading everything we can get our hands on about how to get a toddler to shed the diaper and sit on the throne without causing permanent damage to the child, or the bathroom floor.

During our first tour of potty training duty, Beth read somewhere that you could use Cheerios to potty train little boys. While that made a little sense to me, I suggested to her that candy might be a better bribe to offer. That's when Beth informed me that the Cheerios weren't to eat. The magazine insisted that "floating" Cheerios in the toilet was a great way to motivate little boys to "hit the target," making potty training a fun game instead of an excruciating battle of wills.

Now THAT'S creativity. The diligent man in me had been scolding, instructing, cajoling, pleading, and threatening. For what? Production! "Let's get something done! Let's be efficient! Why are you just sitting there? Work, work, work, work, work so we can both go play, play, play, play, play! C'mon!"

Meanwhile the boys had been, in effect, saying, "Why should I stop playing and go sit in this little room with Mom or Dad demanding a command performance? The way it is now, I can go potty anywhere, any time, without breaking stride. In fact, if we keep doing the diaper thing I can keep doing whatever I want for as long as I want. I can keep having fun."

The creative beauty of the Cheerios solution was that it played both to the man's diligence for the task and the boy's enthusiasm for play. Creativity brought the fun to what needed to be done.

Of course, creativity also opens you up to the new and unexpected. Remember, creativity is combining things in a new way that transforms the ordinary into the original, and you may or may not be completely ready for the original. The Cheerios solution to potty training was wonderful, but there was one day when our oldest son (the one on the back end of potty training) screamed in panic that our younger son (the one on the front end of potty training) was eating Cheerios in the bathroom. My wife came around the corner, assuring the boys that it was okay to eat those Cheerios, but she had some fresher ones in the kitchen. That's when she saw that our fun-loving boy was dropping them in the toilet first, then reaching in and eating them. As I said, creativity breeds originality.

Dancing in the Kitchen

Creativity's power to combine enthusiasm and diligence isn't limited to parenting, either. It can certainly liven up a marriage. Shortly after we moved into our first house, Beth and I were confronted with the task of waxing the parquet wooden floor in our kitchen. We bought the proper wax and applied it to the floor, then read the directions about buffing it to a shine with an electric buffer. We didn't have an electric buffer, and it was almost 10 P.M. when we got to that part of the instructions. With both of us needing to get up and go to work the next morning, we began picturing ourselves on our hands and knees until midnight.

Grudgingly, we got out four or five of my old T-shirts and started to rub. It wasn't long before my aching back and shoulders had enough, and I stood to stretch. Standing there looking at a not-so-fun task, the boy in me hungered for something in this job that I could be enthusiastic about. Then it hit me. I went into the next room and turned on some great, upbeat music. I jumped back into the kitchen, landing my feet on each of the two T-shirts I had left on the floor (and almost breaking my back in the process). There, on the kitchen floor at 10:15 P.M. on a work night, I invited my Cinderella to her feet and gave her two T-shirt slippers. Then we started to dance.

Under normal circumstances, my wife doesn't dance. She's basically shy and a little self-conscious about such things, and until this floor waxing episode we had never really danced together. Why did she dance that night? Well I'm sure it was partly because anything sounded better than buffing a floor on your hands and knees at midnight. But I like to think it also had something to do with the music, the fun, and my enthusiastic (even if left-footed) lead. In fact many times since this encounter, she's responded to my invitation to dance by saying, "Only in the kitchen, and only with you."

By the way, we have an electric buffer now. But sometimes we get the T-shirts out and do some touch-up work—whether the kitchen floor needs it or not.

Jesus and Work and Play

When Jesus was faced with the task of feeding the five thousand, He showed how creatively diligence and enthusiasm can be combined. How many different ways could He have provided food for the crowd? Yet He went about it almost playfully. He sent His diligent, task-oriented disciples into the crowd to find an enthusiastic, fun-loving boy. He merged diligent men who were anxious about the problem with an enthusiastic boy who was excited about the opportunity.

What fun there must have been in seeing that boy's lunch multiply! What a job it still must have been to efficiently pass out all the food and collect the twelve baskets of leftovers! What a creative way to get the job done.

It's a creative approach to our work and our play that gives the boy in us enthusiasm for what the man in us diligently needs to do. Finding that fun in what needs to be done is the key to demonstrating maturity in this most public character arena, and anyone who sees or shares in our work or our play will benefit when we do. How we choose to work and play also gives others a window into the next arena where our character is lived out—the way we make decisions.

Don't Just Take My Word for It

Working and playing like an enthusiastic boy can be good:

Work hard at whatever you do, because there will be no action, no thought, no knowledge, no wisdom in the world of the dead—and that is where you are going. (Ecclesiastes 9:10)

Working and playing like a bored brat is bad:

> *We say this because we hear that there are some people among you who live lazy lives and who do nothing except meddle in other people's business. In the name of the Lord Jesus Christ we command these people and warn them to lead orderly lives and work to earn their own living.* (2 Thessalonians 3:11–12)

———

Working and playing like a diligent man can be good:

> *So let us not become tired of doing good; for if we do not give up, the time will come when we will reap the harvest.* (Galatians 6:9)

———

Working and playing like a task-oriented jerk is bad:

> *Jesus said to them, "The kings of the pagans have power over their people, and the rulers claim the title 'Friends of the People.' But this is not the way it is with you; rather, the greatest one among you must be like the youngest, and the leader must be like the servant."* (Luke 22:25–26)

———

Creativity can balance enthusiasm and diligence in work and play:

> *Whatever you do, work at it with all your heart, as though you were working for the Lord and not for men. Remember that the Lord will give you as a reward what he has kept for his people. For Christ is the real Master you serve.* (Colossians 3:23–24)

Character Trait #2
Responsibility
in Decisions

...Acting with
MIGHT
when you
know what is
RIGHT

A LOCK ON THE GAME

I love playing basketball. My passion for the game is such that I've often walked, run, biked, or driven great distances at odd or inconvenient times just to be part of a pick-up game. I carry two basketballs in the trunk of my car—one for outdoor play and one for indoor play. My gym bag is perpetually packed and waiting with my high-top shoes and other basketball gear. If the phone rang right now, I'd be ready for a game.

That's why it wasn't hard to persuade me to play one summer Sunday afternoon when my buddies called. Time was a little short because I was scheduled to sing a solo during our church's worship service later that evening. My dad, a minister from a nearby town, was to be the guest speaker that night and I wanted to be there in plenty of time. Since the guys who called me to play were from the church basketball team, I figured there would be no problem finishing early enough to get to church.

I was one of the last ones to arrive at the gym, which was on the corporate campus where one of the guys worked. The front door was propped open with a chair, and the normal security guy wasn't at his desk, so I walked on in. As I joined my friends on the gym floor, I also noticed they were playing only by sunlight from the surrounding windows. There appeared to be no electricity.

The guy who was employed there said something about them working on the building this week, and that the place was pretty empty because the facility wasn't really supposed to be open. Apparently only we passionate, dedicated athletes were willing to play under these conditions, because we had the entire gym to ourselves.

The next thing I knew I was in jail being fingerprinted. It seems the gym had indeed been closed for repairs. The couple of guys from our group that got there first had gone around to a back door and opened it with a coat hanger. When the head of security drove by and saw our cars, he was livid. Apparently he was under some pressure because of a couple of incidents on the grounds recently, and not in much of a mood to stretch the rules. He wanted us prosecuted to the full extent of the law. As we were escorted out of the building in our T-shirts and gym shorts, the sheriff's deputies were already arriving. It took three squad cars to carry us all away.

The incident quickly put all of us who were involved into one of two categories: those who were amused by it and those who weren't. Among those who were amused were the sheriff's deputies who hauled us in. They were dribbling our ball down the hallways of the jail, commenting on how dangerous a gang we appeared to be, and asking us whether we were in for stealing passes or playing an illegal defense. Among those who were not amused were our wives, who had to bail us out and go pick up our cars from the impound where they had been towed. Also not amused was my dad, who preached without special music that night because his son was involved in an unexpected prison ministry.

Forks in the Road

As I sat in my gym shorts there at the county jail, I was able to find some consolation in the fact that I personally hadn't known about the coat hanger entrance that afternoon. The guys who did know felt pretty guilty, and the guys who had actually "broken and entered" felt terrible. As they apologized profusely, I found it very hard not to rub their noses in the irresponsible act that had caused all of us so much inconvenience, embarrassment, and expense.

What had they been thinking? At the moment they encountered the locked door, why didn't they just turn away? Did they lose their morality, their judgment, their sense of right and wrong? No, they just made a bad decision. And part of what kept me from assaulting them with "I-can't-believe-you-did-thats" was the quiet, inner realization that I probably would have done the same thing if I had been confronted with the same opportunity.

An opportunity is something that insists on a decision. It's the fork in a road that was previously straight. Sometimes you know the fork is coming, because it's part of the routine road you travel every day. Other times the fork presents itself suddenly—and you have to make a split-second decision based mostly on instinct.

The familiar, predictable forks happen every day. The alarm goes off. You've already snoozed it three times. You squint through bleary eyes at a clock that taunts you with the latest possible hour you've ever slept and still made it to work on time. And you make a decision—probably the same one you've made hundreds or even thousands of times—"I guess I'll go to work today."

Then you go through the various motions and routines that constitute every working day of your life. You arrive safely at your job, and suddenly realize you don't even remember driving there. You've been on auto pilot, yet in the process you've made hundreds of decisions. It may seem there were no forks in the road, that there were no real options in those routines. But then the day comes when you realize you can choose a different route to work, or a different place to work, or a different attitude about work, or a different button that turns the alarm off.

Then there are the unpredictable, unfamiliar forks in the road—the opportunities that you don't know are coming until they stare you in the face. Someone says something in a group at work that you know to be unfair or untrue. One of your spouse's friends tells you she finds you attractive. Your neighbor asks you what you think about God. You go to play basketball and find the gym door locked. Opportunity presents itself. A decision is required.

Decision Doorways

If a guy's work and play are the most visible, public arenas in which his maturity and character are displayed, decisions are certainly an arena almost as public and even more revealing. We all demonstrate our character by the decisions we make. Perhaps more significantly, we help mold and define our character by those decisions.

How many people could you name whose lives have been defined or dramatically altered by one or two key decisions? I could name a bunch. Some were financial decisions. Others were moral, often sexual decisions. Still others were spiritual decisions. In each case, their decisions served them or failed them as a sort of doorway—an entrance into lifelong benefits or consequences.

Have you ever observed two brothers or sisters who, even

though they were from the same parents and same basic circumstances, have turned out practically opposite in character and life direction? Maybe it's true in your own family. How does that happen? The answer, of course, may be as complex or unique as the individuals involved. But chances are you could connect the dots of their life decisions and get a pretty good idea of why the pictures turned out so radically different.

The trouble is that our decision doorways often look a lot alike before we walk through them. I could describe for you three dating relationships I had with three lovely girls and you'd probably have trouble guessing which one became my wife. Yet I'm convinced that two of those relationships would have resulted in tragic marriages. The relationship that did lead to marriage actually had the narrowest doorway by far. But at the time I was in each relationship the doorways looked very similar.

Even when the doorways do look a little different, those very appearances may be misleading. Some of the biggest-looking doorways of decision we face may end up being of little consequence. On the other hand, some of the decisions that seem small or automatic may bring the greatest rewards. Unfortunately, the significance of the doorway is usually at least one step inside.

So how do we take that step? How do we make good decisions when all we have to go on is the outside of the door? The boy in me has a definite answer. Whatever you choose, choose boldly. Make your decisions with passion.

"C'MON, I DARE YOU!"

The boy in us makes decisions based on passion

One of the most pathetic sights in Western civilization is that of a guy being forced to tag along with a woman in a shopping mall. It doesn't matter whether the woman is his wife, girl friend, or mother, the picture is the same. Maybe it's true that on the other side of the world, Chinese women are following five steps behind their men, carrying his burdens with their eyes downcast. But on this side of the world, a lot of American men are trudging along five steps behind their women, carrying her shopping bags with their eyes downcast.

Have you ever wondered why most guys are such terrible, reluctant shoppers? It's at least partly due to the way they make decisions. Guys like making decisions. Women like having options. A guy will walk up to a rack of clothes, spin it once, and pick out what he wants. A woman will spin rack after rack in store after store, then walk out empty-handed and be just as happy as if she'd found something. After all, finding nothing means she gets to spin more racks tomorrow.

Guys seem to get their enjoyment from the benefits of a decision once it's made. Women get half their enjoyment from the process of making the decision, and the other half from telling their friends exactly why they decided what they did.

Maybe it's the traumatic childhood experience of having to try on millions of shoes with our mothers on a Saturday afternoon that has molded us more than we realize. Or maybe we've learned that we might as well make quick shopping decisions because the women in our lives enjoy returning and exchanging things almost as much as they do shopping for new things. Whatever the reason,

CHARACTER TRAIT ● 2

the boy that remains in us still makes us shop like he makes us do so many other things—by making quick decisions based on passion.

A Mouthful of Marshmallows

Have you ever wondered how many miniature marshmallows you could pack into your mouth without swallowing any or blowing chunks of marshmallow across the room? I admit it's a question I had never considered until I was a sophomore in high school. Early in the school year I attended my first Campus Life club meeting, where I learned that humiliating crowd breakers are the pathway to spiritual receptivity.

That particular evening's crowd breaker was a "class competition" to determine which of the four classes could put up the biggest mouth. I still glow with pride to think that I was nominated to represent my class. Actually, my friend Craig had the biggest mouth in our class—he's the one that pushed me to the front, then agreed to be the one pushing marshmallows into my mouth.

The brief moment when I had to decide whether this was a chance to be a champ or a chance to be a chump passed quickly. The girls were cheering, the guys were goading, and a number of rational thoughts were trying to fight their way into consideration. Those thoughts walked away shaking their heads as the line that persuaded me came out of Craig's mouth: "C'mon, I dare you." The whistle blew and the stuffing began.

The first fifty or so weren't too bad. At seventy-five we lost the freshman contender, who was disqualified for chewing and swallowing. When we passed a hundred marshmallows, it was just me against the senior big mouth.

Craig was finding all sorts of creative places and ways to fill my mouth. He was sticking them up between my gums and the inside of my mouth. He was sticking them under my tongue. He was packing them back against what felt like the back of my neck. All the time he was staring hypnotically into my rolling eyes and exploding face, saying, "C'mon, just a couple more, just a couple more . . ."

When number one-twenty went in I had some big-time second

thoughts about my decision. If I looked as stupid and nauseous as the senior in the corner of my eye did, I probably wasn't impressing many girls. I began wondering how much the honor of the sophomore class would benefit from my heroics. I also wondered if anyone had thought about how these marshmallows were getting out of my mouth. I motioned to Craig that I was ready to quit. He said he couldn't understand me with all those marshmallows in my mouth. I thought I was going to be sick. "C'mon, just a couple more . . ." he urged.

I've never been so glad to hear someone else gag as I was when that senior lost his marshmallows—all one hundred and fifty of them. Compassionately, Craig shoved four more in my mouth and declared me the winner. One of that year's many sophomoric questions was answered with a decision of passion. My mouth could hold a hundred and fifty-four miniature marshmallows. And so could the front of Craig's shirt.

The Power of Passion

Passion isn't a bad quality in making decisions, any more than enthusiasm is a bad quality for work and play. In fact, having passion in your decisions is part of what helps us bring enthusiasm to things like work and play. Who wants to work for a boss that thinks maybe this is an okay way, but he's not really sure? Who wants to play for a coach that comes to the huddle with ten seconds left on the clock and says he's considering several options, all of which have a reasonably low chance of succeeding? We all want leaders who are passionate in their decisions, leaders who will say, "Let's do this, let's do it with all our hearts, and let's do it now!"

Passion brings great energy and power to decisions—that's its strength. When the boy in us brings passion to our decisions, we have courage, resolve, even sacrificial will that will not be denied or defeated. No wonder the last hours of Jesus' life have come to be known as His Passion.

The boy in us specializes in passion. He's the one who lets us run hard and play long, even after our body tells us we've had enough. He's the one who lets us say what we think is right, even when it will be unpopular. He's the one who tells us to buy our wife flowers, even though we think they're incredibly impractical. He's the one who lets us cry when we need to.

Even when the boy in us isn't making decisions that are profitable or practical, still he's making decisions that are from his heart, from our heart. And that gives those decisions a certain value all their own.

The Emotional Brat in Us

Of course that pure, boyish passion can also lead to excess, and then once again we discover the brat in us. The problem with passion in decision-making comes when that passion turns into unchecked emotion. That's when the courageous boy in us can become the dangerous brat in us, and even lead us to commit "crimes of passion." When passion in excess is running our decision process, we often endanger ourselves and those around us. We end up choosing pleasure or thrills or mischief or selfish gain, almost always with a short-term view of the outcome.

Bratty passion is often impulsive—it makes us decide hastily, even recklessly, based on the immediate benefits of the opportunity that presents itself. The brat in us seizes opportunities rather than weighing them. He makes decisions to gratify himself rather than to lead and inspire others. He's anxious to take the dare, whatever it is and whatever the odds. The brat in us acts first, then thinks through the consequences of his decisions.

The brat has gone beyond making decisions with passion. He is driven and controlled by passion. He's high on it, and rides it for its thrills. The brat in me is constantly looking for an emotional rush, and makes careless, reckless decisions his hallmark. The passion-driven brat in us loves to say, "I dare you," and wants others to dare him back.

It was on such a dare that I first learned about "chatting porches" when I was in grade school. To "chat" a porch meant to scoop up a handful of gravel (or chat, as we called it) from the roadside and fling it as hard as you could onto someone's big, wooden front porch. The multiple rocks doing multiple ricochets off multiple surfaces could make quite a racket without doing any real damage.

Obviously, chatting a porch isn't something you do to someone you like. And for my friends and me, there was no one less liked than Mrs. G, our sixth-grade teacher. Mrs. G had the reputation of being the "meanest teacher in the school." Of course, that mostly meant she had the strongest discipline in her classroom and the most distant relationship with her students. But the difference between that and being mean is a pretty fine distinction to ask sixth graders to make.

Mrs. G lived between my house and the high school. The fall we were in Mrs. G's sixth-grade class, my best buddy and I walked by her house at least every other Friday night on our way to high school football games. That year, chatting Mrs. G's porch became a traditional part of our evening walk to the game. Her house was almost exactly the halfway point, so we could walk that far hyped on the adrenalin of nervous anticipation, then run the rest of the way to the high school fueled by the adrenalin of terror for our delinquent action.

One memorable chatting night, we had just picked up our handfuls of chat when my buddy asked me to wait a minute—he needed to go to the bathroom. Of course, sixth-grade boys will go to the bathroom almost anywhere, and somehow the edge of Mrs. G's yard seemed an appropriate way to add insult to the injury we were about to impart. So I waited while he made his statement.

As you might imagine, standing there listening to and thinking about my friend's statement while I was shivering and full of adrenalin myself inspired me with the need to make my own statement. So I asked him to wait a minute while I seconded his motion. I was in midstream when he let both handfuls of chat fly.

For a split second before the chat hit I stood there in terror and disbelief, feeling totally vulnerable and more than a little betrayed by my supposed friend. That "friend" was now laughing hysterically at his very practical joke and was in full gallop toward the high school and safety. Then the chat hit.

I don't know if you've ever tried going from that position to a dead sprint or not, but it's not easy. It's also pretty impossible to do without leaving some "evidence" of your mischief on your clothing. I sat through most of the football game that evening with my arms folded in my chilly lap, while my friend went around bragging about his prank. We walked home separately that night. And Mrs. G slept in peace at last, free from at least one boy's bratty, chatty behavior.

Balancing the Boy

At his best, the boy in us decides quickly and boldly. He doesn't hesitate or waver. He reads the situation and makes his call. The boy in me is immune to procrastination.

At his worst, the brat in us decides hastily, impetuously, often using his emotions to the exclusion of his intellect. That's why a guy's decisions, even the quick ones, have to be based on principles as well as passion, and principle-based decisions are the contribution of the man in us.

"MY MIND'S MADE UP"

The man in us makes decisions based on principle

The man in us seeks to govern his decisions by predetermined principles rather than opportunistic passion. Unlike the boy in us, he's very comfortable with rules and regulations. He freely uses words like "always" and "never." The man in us decides to read the instruction manual, while the boy in us longs to start pushing buttons.

The man in us treats decisions differently than the boy in us, because deep down inside he believes that there is a right way and a wrong way, and that only the right way will do. The man in us needs to have all the facts, to understand the guidelines, to see the long-term effects. He can't buy a car without three separate consumer magazines under his arm. He can't choose a movie from the video store without systematically reading every title on the wall. He can't enjoy a magic trick without trying to figure out how it was done. If it can be done by the book, he'll always buy the book.

Deciding to Stop Fighting

Have you ever made the deliberate decision to improve your relationship with someone? Did it work? I remember consciously choosing to change my attitude about a guy who really annoyed me. Chad and I both played basketball at a nearby gym. The nature of our "pick up" games meant that sometimes we'd be on opposing teams and sometimes we'd be on the same team. I hated being on the same team with Chad. In my opinion he loved to shoot, hated to pass, played mediocre defense, and thought he was a lot better than he was. Other than that he was fine.

When we'd shoot free throws at the start of a game to determine teams, I would always shoot after him so I could deliberately miss if he made it, or try hard to make it if he missed. If we were on the same team, he and I didn't talk much and I didn't really enjoy playing. When we were on opposite teams, we almost came to blows more than once.

One day after a series of petty foul calls and barbed words, it finally came to the point where I hated the conflict more than I hated playing with him. I hated the fact that he could determine my enjoyment of the game. I hated avoiding him, and I hated not trying to make every free throw. I knew I couldn't count on him to change, and at the same time I knew my heart and attitude were wrong. So after that game, on the way out of the gym, I decided that whatever it took, I was going to learn to play with Chad, and I was going to learn to like Chad.

The next time we played, we both made our free throws. I didn't really have a plan, but I found one unfolding as I concentrated on liking him. I fed him the ball at every opportunity. When his shot went up (usually immediately), I rebounded ferociously and got the ball back to him. When he made a shot, I complimented him. When his man got away from him, I helped out on defense. By the middle of the game, we were talking some. By the end of the game, our whole relationship had changed. On the way out of the gym that day, I remember lifting my eyes toward heaven and smiling. I had also been praying for Chad. This time my prayer was one of thanksgiving for the power of one little decision.

That's how the man in us makes decisions—deliberately, ahead of time, regardless of feelings. He decides what he will do based on principle, based on what's right, and he presses his decision through to completion.

Whenever there is a principle that can govern a decision, the man in us chooses to reference it, understand it, apply it to reality, and then analyze it afterwards to make sure it worked properly. He sees life as predictable and controllable, and wants to help us make it more and more that way. If anything, the man in us focuses more on the consequences than on the decision itself. If he can predict the end result based on principles, then he can back his way safely into the decision from there. And he much prefers backing into decisions to the boy's way of running into them head on.

To someone who is at all self-conscious, this principle-based man in us might be embarrassing in public. When he's running our decisions, we might ask a smoker in a nonsmoking section to put out his cigarette. We might go into a fast-food place that promises you can "have it your way" and actually special order a catsup-only cheeseburger during the lunch rush. We might complain when the rest rooms aren't clean. We might return a package of underwear that didn't fit right, or use a money-back guarantee over and over and over again until we're satisfied. The principle-based man in us might even convince us to stand in the longer line at the grocery because his eleven items don't qualify for the ten-items-or-less line.

Yes, the principle-based man in us might occasionally be eccentric in his choice of principles, and a little annoying in when and how he chooses to stand for them. But even then he's kind of tolerable, because everyone around him is usually better off when he's trying to do the right thing, and when he's courageous enough to make decisions that match his principles.

Life Directions on 3×5 Cards

It seems as if there are more guys willing to talk about principle-based living than there used to be. Even more encouraging, there seem to be more guys who are willing to try to build their character on eternal principles and then flesh out those principles in their decisions. I want to be one of those guys.

That's why I carry a little stack of twenty-one 3×5 cards with me to work every day and place them by my telephone. Twenty of those cards contain principles or character qualities that I recognize as needing special attention in my life. The twenty-first card contains a short list of people—people to whom I don't feel I'm rightly related for one reason or another. Most of them seem like "difficult" people from my perspective.

Each day as I place that stack of cards by my phone, I pull a new principle to the top of the deck and skim that list of people. Then I decide to pursue that principle and work on those relationships at every opportunity. To be honest, it's hard. I haven't chosen principles that come easily for me or people to whom I'd be naturally drawn. But I'm deciding, based on principle, to improve my character and my relationships inch by inch, day by day.

If you were to watch me attentively during the day, you'd see me shaking my head to myself. That's what I do reflexively when I realize I'm blowing it. I'm not being the person I've decided to be based on principle, and I'm recognizing it in mid-blunder. The man in me is making a decision, and the decision is helping grow me up as a man.

The Rigid Jerk in Me

Like passion-based decisions, principle-based decisions can be taken to an extreme. The security guard that insisted on the arrest and prosecution of our church basketball team, for example, had tilted his principles a little out of balance in my opinion.

When principles are given excessive authority they can become legalistic and even oppressive. That's when the man in us can drift into being the jerk in us. The jerk in us cites principle and letter of the law with no room for exception, tolerance, or compassion. He's only comfortable with what's regulated, agreed upon, enforceable.

To the brat in us, all authorities look like jerks because they put limits on our reckless passion. But to the jerk in us, everybody looks like brats because they're not complying with the rules. They're not living by the principles.

One Way to Pass in Chemistry Class

As early as elementary school we all learned that certain subjects, such as mathematics and science, are governed by precise rules and postulates. Other subjects, say art or literature, are more open to individual interpretation. Anyone's and everyone's opinion was valid when discussing the statement an artist was making, but we were allowed very little latitude in reciting our multiplication tables.

Mr. P, my high school chemistry teacher, was very much a "by the book" sort of teacher. Though he was nearing retirement age, we somehow got the feeling he was still using his lesson plans from his first year of teaching. Those lesson plans were pretty basic: memorize, quiz, memorize, quiz, memorize, quiz. It's the kind of teaching you can get away with in a subject like chemistry, where life is pretty much ruled by the periodic table of elements.

Week after week, we were assigned a certain number of elements off that periodic table, and asked to memorize their chemical abbreviation and valence. On one particular quiz day, I decided to test exactly how routinized and clueless Mr. P really was. I went to the classroom early, before Mr. P arrived with our quizzes, and wrote every assigned element, its abbreviation, and its valence on the chalkboard at the front of the room. In other words, the answers for the day's quiz were available up front on a billboard-sized cheat sheet. Then I drew a box around the answers and wrote "please save" beside it.

Now I know what you're thinking. What kind of teacher would be fooled by such an obvious, juvenile attempt? Apparently one who runs on auto pilot. As the classroom filled with curious and then giggling students, Mr P arrived and picked up the chalkboard eraser. As he reached to routinely erase the chalkboard, I wondered if he'd even notice they were the answers to today's quiz. I wondered if he'd think it was funny, or if he'd want to know who did it.

Then he paused, reading the "please save" request.

"Oh, . . . hmmm!" he said. He then put the eraser down and handed out the quizzes. Several of us looked at each other in disbelief, but nobody said a word. The next day he praised all of us enthusiastically for our near-perfect scores.

Life by the Book

Sometimes when I think back on my prank in Mr. P's class I feel guilty for cheating. Other times I convince myself it wasn't cheating at all—it was playing by the book. If the answers had been written on my sleeve, or on the paper of the person next to me, that would have been one thing. But Mr. P merely asked us to put our books away. He didn't say we couldn't use the chalkboard— the chalkboard whose answers he had preserved for us.

Well, okay, to say that wasn't cheating is obviously an exercise in rationalization. But it does illustrate the weakness in principle-based decisions taken to an extreme. True, the brat in me had made a bad decision on a whim. But the principled Mr. P had become so much of a "roboteacher" that he didn't even recognize the publicly displayed answers to the quiz he was handing out. He wasn't teaching us chemistry, he was dragging us through bland material with rote routines. Easy teaching? Sure. By the book? You bet. Turning kids on to chemistry? Not a chance.

Making decisions solely by the book is the easy way out, and the rule-driven jerk in us knows it. Regardless of the circumstances, the one who benefits most is the one who knows the rule book best. If you can subject every question to a chapter and verse answer, you can use those answers to make your world more predictable and the people around you more controllable.

The rule-driven jerk in us makes us want to manage our work with caution, even fear. He doesn't let us take risks because risks are outside the boundaries. The jerk in us makes us relate to our families with rigid discipline and predictable routines. He doesn't allow spontaneity because then he might lose control. The jerk in us is particularly interested in dominating our authority roles as fathers or bosses because then he can make decisions using his favorite phrases, like: "Because I said so," "I make the rules around here," and "My mind's made up."

Balancing the Man

The man in us who bases his decisions on principles helps us to live a deliberate, value-based life. His thinking is sound and logical, and his decisions are usually easily defensible. The man in us is less susceptible to temptation or passionately reckless behavior because he's able to frame his decisions in the context of what is true or wise over time, not just what seems enjoyable or expedient at the moment.

But we can't go on auto pilot. We can't merely access general principles for our decisions the way a computer accesses its memory banks for data. Too many decisions need heart as well as head. Too many decisions need to fly in the face of logic, or even in the face of established principles. Some principles have stood for hundreds of years before being understood to be wrong. That's why we need both the passion of our heart and the principles of our head to make good decisions. In that balance, our decisions will be more than "right"—they will be responsible.

ACTING WITH MIGHT

When You Know What Is Right

RESPONSIBILITY in Decisions: Passion and Principles in the Balance

A guy who's striving for maturity in his character brings more than reckless passion and more than rigid principles to his decisions. He brings responsibility. Responsible decisions are both principle-based and passion-driven. A responsible guy acts with might when he knows what is right.

Principles are important in decisions because they ground me in what is right. Passion is important in decisions because I need my heart's perspective as well as my head's. That's why James T. Kirk and Mr. Spock always made such a great team on Star Trek. Spock had the logical Vulcan mind; Kirk had the spirited human heart. Together they made responsible decisions and carried out responsible leadership.

Responsible decisions require both private and public courage. The private courage comes as I examine my life principles and choose to hold true to them. The public courage comes when I'm forced to act on those principles with passion and resolve, whatever the cost.

Life-Changing Decisions

Can you point to the most important decision of your life? Perhaps you'd say there were two or three. Whatever those decisions

61

might have been, what roles did passion and principle play?

For me, the most pivotal decision of my life came when I was nineteen. Passion has definitely been running most of my decisions, one of which was to go far away to college and live my life independently on my own terms. The principles by which my parents lived seemed appropriate for them, but too rigid and unreal for me.

My grade school years had been followed by a move to the Chicago suburbs, where I'd found myself in a high school larger than the entire small town in which I'd grown up. Life had turned pretty complex and sophisticated, and by the time my fast-paced adolescence chewed me up and spit me out, I had embraced things like sports, straight A's, and success more than the faithful principles of my roots. My escape to college was exhilarating, and passionate.

That first year away from home presented me with a new set of principles, those held by my professors and my new peers. I began learning the hard way that you can't escape principles, you just decide which ones you will live by. And while the principles my parents stood for tasted stale to me, the principles I was finding on my own began tasting poisonous. Like the Prodigal Son, I had run from the controlling principles of home only to find myself munching on the controlling principles of the swine field. I had to do something. My passion started heating up.

Just when my sense of identity and life direction was reaching the crisis point, God intervened in the form of a faithful friend. By his side at a non-threatening Bible study, I was confronted mercifully with the truth of who Jesus is and what He expects of me in light of who He is. That confrontation with God's Word drove me out into the night, where I walked for hours before stopping on a foot bridge over the little river that ran through campus.

It was as if I was suspended on that bridge between faithful principles and a need for something that was passionately real for me now. There, in the most decisive moment of my life, I poured my heart out to the One who has established all eternal principles and who has bled with eternal passion. And He led me to a responsible decision, one that embraced His principles with a passion that is now uniquely mine.

The Bridge of Responsibility

Responsible decisions are often made on a bridge between principle and passion. Deciding on principle alone can lead us through doors that are sterile, restrictive, uninspiring. Deciding on passion alone can lead us through doors that are selfish, reckless, and dangerous both to ourselves and to others.

Deciding responsibly means acting with might when you know what is right. Knowing what's right means you're deciding based on principles that you've determined ahead of time; you're not yielding to the heat of the moment. Acting with might means that once you understand what's right, you do more than acknowledge it. You decide to passionately and personally pursue the course of action that honors the principles you've found to be true.

It's so easy to simply decide for the path of least resistance, instead of seeking the balance between principles and passion. For example:

> You have a particular weakness, a secret sin if you will. You do battle with it all the time and have asked God to help you overcome your tendency to yield. Today has been a frustrating, stressful day and you're not feeling very moral or committed. An opportunity comes to give in to your weakness. So you decide to seize it. Passion wins. Principles lose. You lose too.

> You've promised your son you'll do something really special with him if he meets certain expectations. He works hard and does his best. He meets almost all the expectations, but falls short in one area. In the meantime, you've over-committed your schedule and have neither the time nor the desire to carry through on the special thing with your son. You tell him you're sorry, but he didn't quite hold up his end of the bargain. Principles win. Passion loses. You lose too.

> You zip into the fast-food drive-through on the way to work for a muffin and a cup of coffee. When you arrive at work, you're putting away the change you stuffed in your shirt pocket and realize the kid gave you change for a twenty instead of the five you gave him. You think about the high prices and poor

service you've often experienced there, and the fact that no-body expects Abe Lincoln behavior anymore. But you decide to drop back by on the way home and give the money back. The kid at the counter acts as if you're an idiot, and has never heard the Abe Lincoln story. Even though it was extra trouble and unappreciated, still you leave feeling good about your decision. Principles win. Passion wins. Because you made a responsible decision, you win too.

Jesus and Decisions

When Jesus was in the Garden of Gethsemene, principles and passion told Him separately not to go to the cross. Principles without passion said that humanity was guilty and deserved what they had coming. Passion without principles said to avoid the pain, the humiliation, the alienation.

But in history's greatest decision, Jesus merged and balanced His principles with His passion. He acted courageously, heroically, passionately on our behalf out of commitment to principles laid down before the foundation of the world.

Responsible decision-making means determining what's right and then acting with might, and those kinds of decisions come neither easily nor automatically. In fact, to make such responsible decisions over and over again requires tremendous strength in the next character arena—the arena of discipline.

Don't Just Take My Word for It

Making decisions like a passionate boy can be good:

> *David, wearing only a linen cloth around his waist, danced with all his might to honor the LORD. And so he and all the Israelites took the Covenant Box up to Jerusalem with shouts of joy and the sound of trumpets.* (2 Samuel 6:14–15)

Making decisions like an emotional brat is bad:

> *Do not deceive yourselves; no one makes a fool of God. A person will reap exactly what he plants.* (Galatians 6:7)

———

Making decisions like a principle-driven man can be good:

> *If you are not willing to serve him, decide today whom you will serve, the gods your ancestors worshiped in Mesopotamia or the gods of the Amorites, in whose land you are now living. As for my family and me, we will serve the LORD.* (Joshua 24:15)

———

Making decisions like a rigid jerk is bad:

> *Stupid people always think they are right. Wise people listen to advice.* (Proverbs 12:15)

———

Responsible decisions are those that balance passion and principles:

> *"Father," he prayed, "my Father! All things are possible for you. Take this cup of suffering away from me. Yet not what I want, but what you want."* (Mark 14:36)

Character Trait #3
Patience
in Discipline

...moving toward
GOALS
while balancing
ROLES

88 KEYS TO DISCIPLINE

On a Sunday morning at 10:00 A.M., when I was seven years old, I decided I would learn to play the piano. It's funny how dream-spawning moments like that can stick in your head. When you want something really badly and then work hard for it, the moment you "set your heart" seems to create a permanent bookmark in your memory. For example, I remember setting my heart on a dream car, a dream vacation, and a dream girl. I've also set my heart on a diploma, a home, and a meaningful relationship with God. Each of these ended up being a commitment whose birth is permanently etched in my memory.

I remember the piano moment so specifically because I remember the event that ignited my motivation. It wasn't a great love for music, or admiration for an outstanding concert pianist. It wasn't that my parents wanted me to take lessons. And it certainly wasn't because of mere opportunity or convenience—in fact, we didn't even own a piano.

No, my inspiration came that Sunday morning in my seven-year-old's Sunday school class when a little guy I hardly knew named Robby claimed he could play the song our teacher was playing. She invited him to the piano, where he sat down and played the piece beautifully. All the kids gathered around him to sing, and the teacher oozed praise all over him. That's when I decided playing the piano was a worthwhile goal.

Of course, I had no concept of what it took to play a musical instrument. I had no idea of the cost or the commitment attached to my impulse. It was definitely one of those passion-driven, boyish decisions. What really lit my fire was the idea of being able to perform—of having people gather around to see what I could do, and then to praise me for it. The piano itself was almost incidental. In retrospect, I guess it's a good thing Robby didn't bring his tuba to class that day.

Biting Versus Chewing

When I approached my parents with the idea of piano lessons, they were cautious. Seven-year-olds are somewhat known for biting off more than they can chew, whether it be paper routes or puppy maintenance. So Mom and Dad began dutifully listing all the obstacles that would have to be overcome if ever I was to "tickle the ivories." The expense, the teacher, the time commitment, the transportation, the competition with schoolwork and play—all were cited. Plus, they too had noticed we didn't have a piano.

One by one, they stacked up painfully realistic obstacles, then capped off what felt like the annihilation of my dream with the classic parental line, "Let's just give it some time and think about it." If there has ever been a one-two punch designed to knock out a boy's dreams, it's that time and thinking combination. I knew it and my parents knew it. In the past, "time" and "thinking about it" had killed everything from new bikes to old horses to sleepovers at mischievous friends' houses. Requiring time and thought was my parents' tried and true method for testing the depth of their seven-year-old's motivation.

I guess their tactic made sense. Opposing an idea like piano lessons outright might mean they'd have to endure the begging, arguing, crying, and other hostile weapons a boy-on-a-mission carries in his arsenal. Time and thinking about it, on the other hand, weren't even fair frontal assault weapons. They were more like slow, silent poisons that just made things go away.

But this dream wasn't going away. Over the next few weeks, I consistently demonstrated my desire to play, and my commitment to do whatever it took to gain the opportunity. As my parents saw my resolve, we together began removing the obstacles that stood between me and piano lessons. Finally we decided that I could begin, walking every day to the church where my dad was pastor to practice on one of the classroom pianos—the same one Robby had played the Sunday morning he lit my fire.

Piano Keys at Fifty Degrees

The next six years were full of ups and downs at the keyboard, as I learned the real connection between the rewards of performance and the rigors of practice. Robby, it turned out, had taken lessons for two years to be able to play that song. Two years is an eternity to a seven-year-old boy.

There were times my motivation intensified, like right after a lesson when I had learned something new or been assigned a neat-sounding piece. (That was in one of the first lessons—they're called "pieces," not songs.) Many other times my motivation was practically snuffed out, like when I had to practice instead of watching TV, or when I was forced to suffer through my weekly lesson even though I hadn't practiced enough.

Not only did my motivation vacillate but the initial obstacles my parents had outlined turned out to be only a partial list. My piano teacher moved across town, making my weekly walk sixteen blocks instead of five. A little girl I loathed scheduled her lesson right after mine, and began showing up early to eavesdrop on my struggles. It seemed every piece I was assigned had some kind of elf, pixie, or fairy in its title—not exactly themes a young boy brags about to his friends when they ask what he can play.

Winter came, and they turned the church's heat down to about fifty degrees to conserve energy. Piano keys at fifty degrees can numb a young boy's fingers pretty fast, especially fingers that have been asked to play a pixie dance with proper expression. They can also numb a boy's motivation. Many were the times I sat scowling at the piano, the pixie, his stupid staccato dance, and the very thought of little Robby, who had stopped coming to church shortly after his piano debut.

Unintentional Discipline

As a seven-year-old boy, I had unwittingly stumbled on to the path where the enthusiastic, passionate boy in me is continually stubbing his toe—the path of discipline. I discovered then, as I continue to rediscover, that discipline isn't something you usually choose to pursue. Nobody really wants discipline for discipline's sake. Instead, you set your sights on something you want, some goal or objective, and then as you start off after it you find that there's a path to follow and a price to be paid. Desire alone, no matter how strong, rarely attains anything more than the most simple and superficial goals. But when I add to my desire things like planning, organization, self-control, and pacing, then I've started down the path of discipline. And try as I may, I find there's no other path to my worthwhile goals.

I desire to lose some weight, but I end up in the disciplines of dieting and exercise. I desire to live in a new house, but I end up in the disciplines of blueprints and financing. I desire to find the girl of my dreams, but I end up in the (dare I be so unromantic?) discipline of dating. I desire to play the piano, but I end up in the discipline of practice.

The arena of discipline in a guy's life runs a little deeper than the arenas of his decisions or his work and play. Whatever is going on deep inside me, I can still put on a show in my work and play that conveys the image I want you to see. I can make a decision that looks good today, then reverse it or wipe it out completely with the decision I make tomorrow, or in private.

But it's not so easy to hide my true character in the arena of personal discipline. My discipline is what takes my decisions and spreads them over time. My decisions will tell you about those things with which I am infatuated. My discipline will prove to you those things to which I am committed.

I can tell you I'm a great tennis player, or teacher, or father. I can decide to start losing weight, or stop losing my temper. I can even tell myself that I'm growing in my spiritual life. But it's the discipline in my life that will eventually tell you and me both the truth.

It's easy to think about discipline in terms of rules, training, organization, and self-control. But that's not where discipline begins. Discipline begins when a goal catches my eye and motivates my spirit. Discipline begins when I set my heart.

Piano lessons and practice sessions themselves weren't attractive to me. And I'd heard the teacher play that song many times before without being impressed. But after Robby played it, the privilege of performance and the promise of admiration and praise motivated me. And that's the great contribution the boy in us brings to the important arena of personal discipline—motivation.

71

"GO FOR IT!"

The boy in us brings motivation to discipline

Newton's first law of motion—the one about inertia—basically says that a guy at rest will stay at rest (usually on the couch) until acted upon by some outside force (usually a woman, but sometimes hunger will do it). In other words, our natural state is doing nothing. That's why we're so compatible with things like TV sports and so incompatible with things like chores and fix-it jobs around the house.

Of course, the flip side of Newton's law is that a guy in motion will tend to stay in motion (usually doing fun things like sports or hobbies) until acted upon by some outside force (again, usually a woman, but sometimes the gravitational pull of the couch is the stopper). That means that once we get started on something it may be hard to get our attention, much less stop us.

That's the great thing the boy in us brings to the arena of discipline—motivation, the go-for-it factor. He's not satisfied with the status quo. He's looking for a new challenge or a worthy goal. He's willing to do things he hasn't done before, often simply because he hasn't done them before. He's also willing to try the things the rest of us are too scared to try. His motivation gives us courage. It can occasionally even get us off the couch.

Making Things Happen

I still remember the words of my high school basketball coach during the award ceremony at the end of our freshman season. In his own gruff way, he was making a special effort to say something personal about each player as we came up to receive our award pins. When my turn to come forward came, he put his hand on my shoulder and smiled.

"Nate," he said, "you're a guy that 'makes things happen' on the basketball court. That's possibly your greatest asset as a player. And you know, sometimes they're even good things."

He got a laugh out of his loaded compliment, but he and I both knew there was real truth in his assessment. My mind flashed back quickly to the tryouts at the beginning of that season. It was not only my first semester in high school but my first semester away from the small town where I'd grown up. Now, lost in the Chicago suburbs and thrown into a huge high school, I had only the faintest glimmer of hope that I could make the grade in any sport.

Encouraged by the fact that the freshman basketball program included not only an A team, but B and C teams as well, I took my glimmer of hope and poured into it the highest octane motivation the thirteen-year-old boy in me possessed. Our high school's gym had been damaged by a tornado over the summer, so tryouts were being held at a neighboring high school from seven to nine-thirty in the evening. For me, that meant rushing home from school, grabbing a quick, non-regurgitable bite to eat, and flying through my homework before heading out the door and into the darkness with my gym bag. Then I had to walk to a nearby shopping mall where I could catch a bus to the school where tryouts were being held.

Arriving at the strange gym, it occurred to me that if I couldn't find the right bus again at 9:30, this small-town boy had no idea what suburb he was in, let alone how to get back to the one where he reluctantly lived. I looked around in the sea of 150 freshman faces for a familiar, or at least friendly one. Nope. This wasn't going to be easy. My high-octane motivation was siphoning off fast.

Things got worse. The head coach announced that guys who had played last year at one of the junior highs he listed should move to one end of the court. All others should move to the other end of the court with the assistant coach. Then he read off a list of junior highs that of course didn't include mine.

I was crestfallen. Even a freshman in high school could figure out which end of the floor was going to have the coaches' attention. My junior high was 350 miles from here, and not on anybody's list.

What chance did I have to play at the right end of the court?

I shuffled down to the dream cemetery and looked around at my fellow corpses—the guys with whom my basketball career would probably end. I couldn't help but get a little mad at the unfairness of the tryout procedures, and that spark of anger must have ignited the octane in my near-empty motivation tank. I decided to go out with a blaze of glory. It was time to make something happen.

The next few minutes I played like a boy possessed. I stole a pass, made a lay-up, hit an outside shot. I hawked the poor guy I was guarding with probably the most furious defense I've ever played—before or since then. I dived on the floor for loose balls. I went after every rebound. I was intensely motivated. A few minutes later, I was invited to play at the other end of the floor.

My mind flashed back to the award ceremony and the coach's comment about my "making things happen." After that tryout session, I had gone on to make the "A" team, to lead the starting five in steals and assists, and come in second in scoring. Even more important to me, I had become part of a winning team of guys who in turn became my friends. And it all started when a scared thirteen-year-old boy took a little motivation and lit a fire in his belly. I could hardly wait to see what things I might be able to "make happen" as a sophomore. Some of them might even be good things.

Victory Over Apathy

I can't fully describe the motivation it took for that thirteen-year-old boy to even go to those basketball tryouts. A big, loud, frightened part of me said to stay home and watch TV that night. Is it exaggeration to say that getting off the couch and walking out into the dark was one of the most courageous things I've ever done? Maybe not. As an adult, I don't get many opportunities to overcome that kind of uncertainty and self-doubt anymore. There aren't as many desperate situations where all I can do is muster some motivation and "make something happen." But when those rare opportunities do come along, when the status quo is unacceptable but change is scary, that's when I rely on the boy in me.

It's the motivated boy in us who helps us endure the hardships of discipline, and without the hardships of discipline, there's little chance for growth or maturity. I know lots of basically diligent people who "started" taking piano lessons. I know others who "started" learning a foreign language, or jogging every day, or undertaking a difficult job. But somewhere along the line, they lost their motivation.

It didn't seem to matter if they had the skill or time or knowledge or personal organization to finish what they started. Those things could have played an important role in their success, just as a railroad track plays a role in the success of a locomotive. But the track is of little value if there's no fire in the engine's belly.

When the boy in us sets his sights on a goal, he can bring powerful, powerful motivation with him. During the years I played organized basketball, I endured seven seriously sprained ankles, two knee operations, and a mild concussion. I ran countless wind sprints, shot innumerable free throws, and endured the impatient, often cruel scorn of fans who liked winning better than losing.

Looking back, it amazes me to recall the suffering and sacrifices I fought through in order to play basketball. Yet on the second day of sophomore football tryouts I quit the team because an assistant coach yelled at me. Discipline needs sufficient motivation, or it won't endure.

The Reckless Brat in Us

As powerful and good as motivation can be, there is such a thing as unbridled motivation, and that's where the boy in us starts yielding to the brat in us. The brat in us basically says, "I want it NOW, and I don't care who or what is standing in my way." He wants instant results, instant success, instant gratification.

In his bestselling book *The Seven Habits of Highly Effective People*, Steven Covey defines maturity as the ability to delay pleasure or satisfaction. The brat in us is anything but mature. He's impatient, not only with his family and his employees but with road construction, slow restaurant service, and most of the U.S. government. He judges all these primarily by how fast they are or aren't moving. His impatience is theoretically with their gross inefficiency, but what's really bothering him is how much they're slowing down his progress toward his goals or desires.

The brat in us is lustful. He sees something he wants and he takes it. Maybe he only takes it in his thoughts, or maybe he waits until he can act undetected. But he doesn't take "wait" for an answer, and you never tell him "no."

Bratty motivation works against true discipline, because it lacks pacing or restraint. The brat in us would rather covet than set goals. He'd rather envy than learn responsibility. He'd rather steal than earn. He'd rather act than think.

When our motivation gathers a full head of steam and starts rolling along toward its desired goal, its unchecked power and momentum can be dangerous. Often no one will challenge the steamrolling brat in us, because willfulness can be mistaken for positive traits like faith or courage, and those who are pressing ferociously toward a goal often appear heroic, even if their goal is leading them over the edge of a cliff. Those who would warn of the impending danger, however, risk the defensive wrath of the willful one and even the jeers of his naive supporters who think he's just following his dream.

Terrorists and warped religious leaders are brats. They've let intense motivation of some kind overtake and control their wills, and in following that intense motivation they can take lots of people over the cliff with them. At given times in history, certain terrorists have been labeled heroes, and certain crooked religious leaders have been labeled prophets or martyrs. Why? Because they appeared to have zeal, patriotism, faith, or courage, when actually they just wanted something very, very badly.

Sometimes we're brats too, when we let our goals or our desires become so important and consuming that we exercise no restraint, self-control, planning, or pacing in our path toward fulfilling them. Others may call us determined or "high-energy" or ambitious. They may even admire our resolve or our willingness to sacrifice. If they're not asking what our real goal is or what our real motives are in seeking that goal, they may not recognize the brat in us, and may unwittingly cheer him—and us—over the edge of the cliff.

The Brat in Love

Did you ever have a friend your parents didn't completely like or trust? Worse yet, did you ever date someone your parents couldn't completely . . . stand to look at? I dated a girl one time that my parents basically liked as a person, at least initially. At the same time, they were concerned that we were getting much too serious. As their concern increased, my motivation to be with this girl all the time was building to steamroller intensity.

In retrospect, I don't envy my parents' position. Have you ever felt compelled to tell someone close to you that you think they're in a problem relationship? Unless it's handled perfectly, confronting that situation can be like lying in the path of the steamroller. There's little chance of diverting its path, and opposing its determined course of action can leave you looking and feeling like a well-intentioned pancake.

Fortunately, a series of circumstances brought about the end of the relationship without my parents ever having to lie in the path of their teenager's emotionally charged, romantic motivation. The hurt that was necessary to break the relationship was severe, but my parents were spared from having to play a part in it. Later, however, as they told me of their deep concern and relief that things had worked out the way they had, I was able to see things more objectively. I saw then how fortunate everyone was that the relationship had ended, but I realized too that if they had stood in the path of my motivation at the wrong time, the brat in me wouldn't have been denied.

If the relationship had gone on, there may have come a time when those who cared about me would have had to stand in front of my willful, steamrolling motivation. But if you've ever had to make that stand, you know it isn't easy. And you probably still have the brat tracks up your back to show for it.

Balancing the Boy

At his best, the boy in us sets our heart on something and gives us the motivation to get started on the path of discipline. He helps us escape the status quo and set our sights on the end result we want. The boy in us has a vision for what can be.

At his worst, the brat in us tells us to plow ahead without regard to the consequences. He can go off half-cocked in a dozen different directions and frustrate progress in all of them. That's why to be truly disciplined, a guy's motivation has to be balanced with caution, and caution is the contribution of the man in us.

"NOT SO FAST . . ."

The man in us brings caution to discipline

The Best Ticket in Town

There's no feeling in the world like the feeling your stomach gets when you first spot flashing red lights in your rearview mirror. The last time I experienced that wonderful adrenalin rush was on the way to a noon workout. Things had been particularly hectic at work that morning, and as I left for the gym I debated whether I should even take time out for the exercise. I was in a hurry, and well, okay, maybe the light was a little more orange than yellow when I went through it. That particular traffic light was one of three in a row that were only a few car lengths apart. They all change at about the same time, and I'm pretty sure I hit at least one of them green and one of them yellow. But the third one . . . well, I have to admit that the whole color scheme of that experience is still a little blurry to me.

I do know that red was the last color I saw, and that the officer didn't really care to talk about gradations of color. He did, however, suggest that I could discuss reds and yellows with a judge friend of his at a future date. Then he took my license in lieu of the $75 I didn't have, and left me with the option of paying that fine later or meeting him and his friend in court.

As I drove away, my indignation, embarrassment, and frustration were quickly replaced with a tremendous sense of caution. The kind officer had explained to me that if I paid the fine by mail and had no further infractions for ninety days, the incident would not go on my driving record and affect my insurance rates. I decided that was the best option, all things considered, yet somehow it immediately transformed my driving habits into those of my great-grandmother. For the next ninety days, I drove with my hands in the textbook "10 and 2" position. I read and obeyed each speed limit sign with care. I came to a complete and total stop at each red octagon. I signaled each and every lane change, sometimes miles in advance. And I stopped at every single traffic light, sometimes even the green ones.

Yellow Lights of Caution

My newfound caution on the road sometimes annoyed the less than cautious boys who found themselves driving around me. But ninety days later my discipline paid off and my driving record was clean again. Not only that, something seemed to permanently change inside me after getting that ticket. I may not be as annoyingly cautious as I was during those first ninety days, but I'm convinced I've become a safer driver. My ticket experience gave me a greater sense of caution, which in turn made me a more disciplined driver.

The man in us contributes most to our personal discipline when his wealth of experience results in more cautious thoughts and habits. What has made me a safer driver is not a fear of yellow lights, but an earlier recognition of the rewards and consequences that go with them. I don't approach a yellow light now without thinking about that ticket and the consequences of making a poor decision. My disciplined mind is quicker and therefore my response is smarter, not because I had one bad experience, but because of how that experience taught me to think and act.

It makes sense that the man in us brings caution to our personal disciplines, because he's the part of us that looks at past experiences and seeks to learn from them. The motivated boy in us is anxious to create a new experience, so he's willing to make some mistakes in order to make some progress. But the man in us looks more at the scars from our past mistakes, and sees that careful, deliberate action could have helped avoid them.

It's that weathered and worn experience that gives the man in us a sense of context and perspective, and these are extremely helpful in the arena of discipline. The man in us has had a speeding ticket or two, so he doesn't drive so fast. He's kissed a few girls, so he knows how to avoid bumping noses. He's been betrayed, so he knows better who he can trust. He's been rejected, so he reads the signals more carefully before he takes risks.

The man in us who is cautious in his disciplines is very compatible with the man in us who makes decisions based on principles instead of passion. In fact, one principle-based decision after another is what helps create a life of personal discipline that is very cautious and controlled. In turn, that kind of cautious personal discipline is what enables us to make decisions based on principle rather than in the heat of the moment.

The Balancing Act

I haven't spent a lot of time at the circus, but I have seen enough tightrope walkers to make one generalization about them. They're not in a hurry. Even though they've spent hours and hours of practice, even though they have years of tightrope experience, even when they're working with a safety net—you just can't seem to rush them.

Unlike the proverbial chicken crossing the road, a circus acrobat doesn't walk a tightrope just to get to the other side. There are much quicker and safer means of accomplishing that objective. No, the acrobat's main concern is with balance. He's out to demonstrate, first of all, how well he can control his own weight and motions, and then to add things like unicycles, blindfolds, and juggling just to prove his skill. Throughout the entire act balance is his highest priority, and that makes caution his greatest friend.

Like the circus acrobat, the man in us tends to see our life as an incredible balancing act. Even the simplest of lifestyles requires balancing a job, friendships, finances, leisure and time, and often we add unicycles like marriage, children, church commitments, and then try to juggle hobbies, community service, maybe a second job . . . and the list goes on and on.

The man in us sees himself as employee, boss, husband, father, friend, investor, coach, churchman, yard worker, sports fan, and more. So when anyone—especially the motivated boy in us—says,

"Let's try something else!" the man in us may react with anything from realism to outright fear. And whatever is driving his reaction, his way of dealing with it is usually the same—caution.

The boy in us says, "Let's build something!" The man in us counts the cost before buying the first nail. The boy in us hates to wait. The man in us is very comfortable waiting, especially if the other option is rushing in hastily. The man in us likes a long view of things. He can respond positively to ideas, dreams, and goals, but is much more comfortable when they can be framed in terms of plans, schedules, and budgets. He'd rather work in the accounting department than the sales department.

The Fearful Jerk in Us

If you've ever driven behind someone who's going 20 m.p.h. below the speed limit in the passing lane, or driven with someone who insists on parking "for safety" a mile from the nearest entrance, you know that caution can be taken to an extreme. When the man in us gets so cautious that he quenches the motivation in us, then he's gone too far. He's become the jerk that destroys our goals and dreams rather than bringing caution and discipline to them.

While the brat in us might ruin our goals by driving them too fast, the jerk in us cages them up with caution that turns into paralyzing fear. In fact, the jerk in us has a cage full of trips never taken, books never written, proposals never made, business ventures never financed. The more tragic victims in his cage can be words never spoken, letters never penned, risks never taken, relationships never kindled.

The overly cautious jerk in us procrastinates. He says things like, "Maybe some day . . ." or "That's too extravagant . . ." or "You don't know how she'd react . . ." or "Better not risk it." He's not just cautious about consequences, he fears them. For the jerk in us, the rewards never outweigh the risks. Change never offers more than sameness. Dreams, goals, and motivation threaten and challenge the status quo. And he can't allow that.

Dating for Six Years

The overly cautious man in me came dangerously close to making me lose the girl of my dreams. When my wife and I started dating in college, the motivated boy was definitely in charge of whatever discipline there was in our relationship. At times, the reckless brat in me even took over. But as I approached graduation a year ahead of her, the man in me brought some wise caution to our plans. I should find a job. She should finish school. We should save some money. Then we could talk about the future.

But the longer we yielded our relationship to caution, the more control the cautious, fearful man in me seized. He was concerned with the number of things I was balancing—a full-time job, a part-time job, managing my own apartment, paying my bills—and maintaining a long-distance relationship seemed hard enough without talking about deeper commitment.

The man in me also knew I had an extremely high regard for marriage, and cautiously urged me to make sure it was "right" before diving in after only six years of dating. After all, he had seen me still looking at other girls. He knew my reservations about whether things were "perfect enough" in this relationship. He had balanced my checkbook. He had counted my unfulfilled goals. He knew how much marriage could change and complicate things.

You know the overly cautious man in you has gained too much control when your normally conservative family and friends are urging you to act rather than cautioning you against acting too hastily. Usually parents are saying things like, "Don't rush into anything. You have your whole life ahead of you." Or, "Don't you think you two are getting a little too serious?"

In my case, friends and family were saying, "What are you, crazy? She's an incredible, beautiful, wonderful girl! What on earth are you waiting for??" My tongue-in-cheek response was usually that I was waiting for "a sign" or something. In fact one night I returned home and upon opening the living room drapes found a huge banner with lightening bolts painted all over it. *"Nate, Beth is THE ONE!"* it screamed. A couple of my overly zealous friends had gone to a lot of trouble to get across the message that everyone around me was thinking, whispering, or shouting. Don't be so cautious, or you're going to lose her.

It was, in fact, the prospect of losing her that ended up rattling my cautious cage. After a number of "we're just not sure" crises, Beth issued an uncharacteristic ultimatum. She didn't want us to see each other anymore until we were sure we were ready for a commitment. Apparently her patience had run out after only six short years.

If anything can liberate the cautious man in us from the paralysis of his fear, it's the threat of tragic loss. We get motivated to bid more for that dream car or house if we think someone else is going to buy it. We get motivated to take that trip, or start that business, or apply for that new job if we believe it's now or never. We get motivated to spend more time at home if we sense our family is slipping away.

When Beth presented me with the prospect of losing our relationship for good—of losing her for good—motivation returned. The boy was back in town. On the wall at our wedding reception was a large paper banner with lightning bolts on it. I guess even the cautious man in me knew enough to save it for the right occasion.

Balancing the Man

The great thing about the cautious man in us is that he knows how to use words like "wait" and "no," which rarely invade the vocabulary of the motivated boy in us. As a result, the cautious man in us saves our necks countless times, probably more than we even realize. After all, he's only looking out for our well-being. He knows we're busy, that we're balancing a lot of roles that compete with an already full slate of goals, and he wants us to count the cost before building the tower.

But we can't let him paralyze us. We can't let him keep us from dreaming or from risking. We can't let him cage us up with fear. True productive discipline in life comes when the cautious man in us is balanced with the motivated boy in us. When that's happening, our personal discipline will be governed by a critically important character trait—patience.

MOVING TOWARD GOALS

While Balancing Roles

PATIENCE in Discipline:
Motivation and Caution in the Balance

Discipline begins with motivation. Not until we've truly set our heart on something do we have the energy, resolve, or courage to take the first step.

Discipline is guided by caution. If we respond to every motivation that hits us, we'll scatter in a hundred different directions, many of them worthless, many of them dangerous.

Discipline in the balance requires patience. Patience is the character trait that lets us govern our motivation and balance our many roles with appropriate caution, and thus make steady, enduring progress toward our goals. Patience is what lets us endure the difficulties, setbacks, and especially the distractions that are bound to stand in the way. Patience enables us to sit down and draw from our experience and the counsel of others in order to solve the problems frustrating our discipline. Patience lets us thoughtfully evaluate and reevaluate why we're doing what we're doing, and thereby rekindle motivation when it subsides.

A Worthwhile Walk

Our family has grown to love the mountains of Colorado. When we're on vacation there, one of my favorite things to do is get up early in the morning and walk. Far away from the routines and problems of everyday life I can think, pray, plan, and reset my perspective. Though it's usually a struggle to get up early when you're on vacation, my walking time in the mountains is one of the few things I've found to be worth the sacrifice.

One summer we stayed at a friend's place that offered a nearby dirt road up to a majestic overlook. Each night I would go to bed almost giddy at the thought of getting up early the next morning and walking through the pristine mountain air to the tranquil spot overlooking a glassy lake. There I could sit on a rock and see clearly for miles. Somehow it seemed I could see life more clearly from up there, too.

I was on my way down the mountain one morning when I heard a low, rumbling growl. I looked up to meet the steely eyes of a large, wolflike dog. Not wanting to show him any fear, I smiled one of the pleasant smiles I had left over from my tranquil time on the mountain. He didn't smile back. I looked at his tail—not a wag. I decided to circumvent my adversary at a reasonable distance and keep walking, sure that the farther past his turf I got the less he'd care about growling at me.

I underestimated how much he cared about growling at me. He also cared a great deal about following me, snarling at me, getting closer and closer to me, and then just as I turned to see how close he was getting—he bit me. That's right. He bit me! Actually it was more of a snap than a bite, but teeth are teeth!

I was no longer having a tranquil mountain experience. Every Jeremiah Johnson or Grizzly Adams movie I had ever seen came racing into my head. Suddenly it was civilized man against wild, attacking beast in a survival of the fittest. Man the vacationer had become man the prey, and frankly, I was more than a little scared.

I spun around and screamed, and while the wolf (he stopped being merely a dog in my mind shortly after he bit me) reacted, I ran to the roadside and grabbed a baseball-sized rock in each hand. The wolf appeared to be acquainted with the concept of stoning, because he did back off as I repeatedly pump-faked my rocks at him. He continued following me for a few hundred feet, snarling and barking, then turned away. I ended up backpedaling the rest of the way down the mountain.

Giving Up or Going On

By the time I returned to my family, the wolf had become a dog again and my adrenalin-charged fear had subsided into nervous concern. Might he come around the place we were staying? Was it safe for our kids to be outside? Where was that dog's owner? The place where I met the dangerous dog was far enough away from the house that most of these questions were irrelevant. But the question that wouldn't go away was whether or not I'd try to walk up the mountain again.

That may seem like a silly little concern. There are lots of mountains in Colorado, and lots of different directions I could have walked to avoid that dog. But that place of tranquil beauty had become almost sacred to me, and whether or not an unchained dog would keep me from returning there became an issue of principle. Motivation said walk the mountain. Caution said stay away from that dog. Patience said find a way to walk the mountain safely.

Four Cookies and a Big Stick

The next morning I started out the door with four cookies wrapped up in my pocket. On my way up the mountain I located a good-sized walking stick, one that probably wouldn't break easily over a dog's head. By stick or by cookie, I was getting past that dog and going up the mountain. I passed the several cabins that dotted the road up to the overlook, but saw no sign of the dog.

As I sat on my rock that morning, my thoughts turned to the story of David and Goliath, toward matters of courage and resolve, toward goals that are worth risks and dangers that are worth caution. Though that overlook spot had always been special, somehow it had more value that morning than ever before.

On the way down the mountain I saw the dog. This time he was by the front door of one of the cabins, and a man was coming out of the cabin as I walked by. I went over to the man, introduced myself, and asked him about the dog. He was shocked to hear of the incident, and apologized profusely. The dog was docile and friendly—he almost seemed apologetic too. I fed him a cookie.

The rest of that vacation I walked the mountain every morning.

And each time I passed that cabin, I remembered what it felt like to want something badly, to be hindered from it to the point of personal danger, and then to patiently discipline my intense motivation with prudent caution, finding a way to press on. I remembered a friend who was undergoing chemotherapy. I thought of people in other lands whose faith walked a much more serious path than mine every day. Even though I only saw the dog a couple of times from a distance, I continued to carry cookies and a big stick with me. But now they were more for me than they were for the dog.

Counting the Cost

Worthwhile walks almost always demand patient discipline. We guys know that in our heads because we see it over and over in sports, in work, in parenting. But often the gap that exists between what our hearts want and what our lives deliver is the simple yet profound gap of discipline.

We want a trim, healthy body, but we aren't disciplined in exercise or diet. We want a loving, exciting marriage, but we aren't disciplined in creating quality time or communication. We want happy, obedient children, but we aren't disciplined in mentoring or setting boundaries. We want a growing, deepening spiritual life, but we aren't disciplined in our intake of God's Word or our outpouring of ministry and service. In each of these cases, the challenges may be ones of motivation—wanting it enough to set our heart on it, or caution—counting the cost and crafting a reasonable plan to get there.

There's no magic formula for discipline. That's why patience is so important in its development. Without patience we can't balance all the things that cry for our attention and still make progress toward the things we've determined are important. Discipline comes with patience and patience has opportunity to develop as we encounter obstacles to our goals. We then respond either with motivation or with pouting and recklessness. We respond either with caution or with fear and apathy. If we let them, our experiences will both teach us and transform us. If we won't be taught or transformed, we'll be spoiled or paralyzed, because we didn't stay under the pressure long enough to mold our character.

A Small Blue Dot

While there are no magic formulas or shortcuts to patient discipline, there do seem to be key devices in its development. Those devices we might simply call "reminders."

In the middle of my right hand's palm is a small blue dot. I received it when I was a small boy, at the home of a dear neighbor I knew as "Ebbie." Ebbie lived across the street from us, and would frequently invite me over to play Old Maid—a card game I thought she had invented. Of course now I understand that Ebbie invited me over as a favor to my mom, who either needed to go somewhere or just stay home and take a rest from me. But Ebbie never made me feel like she was baby-sitting. She made me feel like I was her friend.

Ebbie and I would sit on the floor together for hours and play what must have been a very monotonous game for her. She'd give me a pencil and paper and let me keep track of who had won the most games. I remember thinking she wasn't very good at Old Maid for someone who had invented it, because I always seemed to win more often than she did.

One day as I was leaving her house I tripped and fell, landing on the pencil I had left in the middle of the floor. I lifted my little hand to find that the pencil's sharp tip was imbedded in my palm. Ebbie quickly pulled it out and took care of me, shedding more tears than I did over the relatively harmless accident.

Surprisingly, that blue dot in the center of my right palm is still there. It's lasted all these years, and has continued to serve as a reminder. Certainly it reminds me of Ebbie's house, the pencil accident, and playing Old Maid. But it also reminds me of Ebbie's life and character. It reminds me that an authority can be a friend. It reminds me that I want to be the kind of person who sits on the floor with people who can give me very little in return. Each elderly hand I shake at church or hold at a hospital bedside now receives the hand—and the heart—that Ebbie's pencil marked for me.

Reminders can be powerful things in developing a life of discipline. I look at the faded trunk of my repainted car and I remember the near fatal collision that's made me a more disciplined driver, and a more thankful child of God. I look at my wedding ring and I remember to schedule a "date night" with the girl of my dreams that I sometimes take for granted. I look at the snapshot in my wallet and I remember to plan an event that makes my family feel as important as my job. I look at the Bible on my nightstand and I remember how much my life wobbles when I don't spend some serious time there.

Yes, the patiently disciplined man in us does well when he surrounds himself with things that remind him of his goals and dreams, and help him control and regulate his life accordingly. Those reminders may be written statements, pictures, symbols of commitment, or even scars. When he's down, they motivate him. When he's out of control, they caution him. When he's patient, he stops long enough to notice those reminders, and to discipline his behavior to honor the commitments for which they stand.

Jesus and Discipline

When Jesus was at His peak of popularity, crowds followed Him wherever He went. His disciples, like all would-be "handlers," were trying to protect Him from distraction and plot a course of successful messiahship. Yet in the midst of their efforts, the disciples could hardly turn their heads without Jesus challenging them with some unexpected behavior.

The disciples would be shooing children away, and Jesus would scoop one up on His lap. The disciples would want to walk miles out of their way to avoid Samaria, and Jesus would initiate a noonday conversation with an adulteress there. The disciples would value their sleep, and Jesus would get up well before daybreak to commune with His Father.

Clearly Jesus was motivated in ways the disciples didn't fully understand, and was careful about details they didn't recognize as important. Yet with patient, godly discipline He balanced the many demands on His life and His many roles. And all the while He moved with unwavering motivation toward Jerusalem, and a hill called Golgotha. What patience, both with His disciples and with His sojourn.

Patience in discipline can help us move toward the goals we know to be important while balancing the many roles life requires us to play. It can help us hit our targets in work and play. It can help us make wise, responsible decisions. And when patient discipline is at its best, it even has power over the next character arena—how we choose to communicate.

Don't Just Take My Word for It

Having discipline like a motivated boy can be good:

> *David said to Saul, "Your Majesty, no one should be afraid of this Philistine! I will go and fight him."* (1 Samuel 17:32)

Having discipline like a reckless brat is bad:

> *Jesus went on to say, "There was once a man who had two sons. The younger one said to him, 'Father, give me my share of the property now.' So the man divided his property between the two sons. After a few days the younger son sold his part of the property and left home with the money. He went to a country far away, where he wasted his money in reckless living. He spent everything he had. Then a severe famine spread over that country, and he was left without a thing."* (Luke 15:11–14)

Having discipline like a cautious man can be good:

> *Your insight and understanding will protect you and prevent you from doing the wrong thing. They will keep you away from people who stir up trouble by what they say—men who have abandoned a righteous life to live in the darkness of sin.* (Proverbs 2:11–13)

Having discipline like a fearful jerk is bad:

> *So do not start worrying: "Where will my food come from? or my drink? or my clothes? (These are the things the pagans are always concerned about.) Your Father in heaven knows that you need all these things."* (Matthew 6:31–32)

———

Patience balances motivation with caution:

> *May you be made strong with all the strength which comes from his glorious power, so that you may be able to endure everything with patience. And with joy give thanks to the Father, who has made you fit to have your share of what God has reserved for his people in the kingdom of light.* (Colossians 1:11–12)

Character Trait #4
Love
in Communication

...saying what's
TRUE
with encouragement
TOO

SAYING THE "L" WORD

How does a guy tell a girl that he loves her?

The answer to that question, of course, is subject to any number of variables—the personality of the guy, whether or not the girl reciprocates his love, how long they've known each other—even the guy's age. For instance, "I love you" will probably be expressed differently depending on whether the guy is eight, eighteen, twenty-eight or eighty-eight.

For the eight-year-old, giving the beloved a good shove in the back during recess will do. For the eighteen-year-old, just stammering the words out loud while staring at your shoes may be enough, perhaps with a long-stemmed rose as a chaser. By the time you're twenty-eight you definitely have to consider saying it with jewelry, usually the kind that comes with monthly payments.

And at eighty-eight? Well, Jay Leno once commented on how many elderly married couples seemed to die within a couple of months of each other. Was their love for each other so strong that they just couldn't go on alone? No, Jay answered, that's a myth. Whichever spouse died first simply forgot to tell the other where they left the medication. Expressions of love do change with the seasons of life.

I was closer to that eighteen-year-old stage when my relationship with Beth blossomed into love. We had met during the Fall semester at college, and by Thanksgiving break I was totally "whipped." She seemed to be looking pretty starry-eyed herself, and I thought she probably felt the same way about me as I did about her.

Getting there hadn't been easy, though. In going away to college, Beth had left a hometown boyfriend behind. By the end of freshman orientation weekend she had already turned down the advances of several upperclassmen, and made it clear she wasn't interested in being courted. So by the time I noticed her beautiful smile and asked about her, several of those rejected male egos were quick to tell me "not to bother."

Still I was more than a little mesmerized by her, and decided I had to at least get to know her better. I started by concocting a survey of incoming freshmen to be published in the school newspaper. That gave me the opportunity to sit at an official table during registration and "interview" freshmen (and freshwomen) as they completed their class scheduling. Most of the freshmen I quickly asked three "yes or no" questions. But by the time Beth left my table I also knew her name, hometown, dorm room number, roommate, class schedule, and general interests. I also knew she was taking a class I had taken the previous year. When I offered to save her the $30 textbook fee by loaning her mine, she agreed to meet me later at the coffee shop to pick it up. Love means never having to say you're sorry for the desperate measures you use in winning the girl of your dreams.

In the days and weeks that followed, I did everything in my power to remove that hometown boyfriend from Beth's thoughts. I hung around the campus post office for hours at a time waiting for her to come by. I found out when she ate lunch and dinner and adjusted my schedule accordingly. I attended events that only freshmen usually attended. When Beth went back home in mid-October, she was ready to tell old what's-his-name she had met someone else. By the time she got ready to go back home for Thanksgiving break, I was ready to tell her I loved her.

That Magic Moment

The afternoon Beth was to depart, my stomach was all in knots. In fact, it had been in knots on and off for over a week. I had said the words "I love you" before, but the way I was feeling now made me wonder if I had ever really meant it. Part of me was confident she wanted to hear those words. Another part reminded me that I had always been the one running out ahead in this relationship. I still had BHTBWD memories (before hometown boyfriend was dumped) of the days she wouldn't even hold my hand. My head said that three months wasn't a very long time—why not wait a little longer and make sure? My heart said that if I didn't tell her today I'd explode. On this particular day, the heart won.

After helping her load her luggage into her car, I asked Beth if she had time for a quick walk. She checked her watch nervously, reminding me that she had a five-hour drive ahead of her. Then, reading the sick puppy disappointment in my face, she smiled and said we could walk for a little while. Halfway across campus, I pulled her out of the cold November air into the campus chapel. It seemed that what I had to say was almost holy, and the chapel seemed like a good spot. I needed a quick, silent prayer anyway. I told her that I needed to tell her something before she went away— something that was very important. She looked almost as nervous as I did, but told me to go on. Then I did it. I told her I loved her.

It was as if a dam had burst in my heart. I had taken the risk. I had bared my heart and soul for her. I had been the first to use the "L" word. Now all that remained was for her to reciprocate. I had done the hard part, all she had to do was echo. She smiled, then her lips parted. *Here it comes,* I thought. *What a memory-making magic moment this is.*

Then Beth simply replied, "Thank you."

The Leap of Communication

Thank you? THANK YOU??!! What kind of response is that to "I love you?" I was almost too surprised to be disappointed, though I tried not to show it at the time. I walked Beth to her car, and watched her drive away. She had five hours to bask in the fact that I loved her. I had a long holiday weekend to puzzle over why she said "thank you" instead of "I love you."

Communication is an exhilarating undertaking. When you choose to communicate (and it is a choice), you take something that's been brewing inside you—something that's a part of who you are and what you're feeling or thinking—and give it expression. More than that, you give it away to someone else, and their acceptance of it then gives it new life. Lots of things brew inside our heads and hearts that never get communicated, and as a result many of those things die. But once they are communicated, once they're re-created in someone else's mind and memory, they have the capacity to change and transform.

It's true that some of our communication is flippant, casual, in some cases even thoughtless. But even then we're unleashing something more powerful than we realize. Our words tell a great deal about our internal condition, whether we intend them to or not. They also have a great influence over the people and world around us, whether we intend them to or not.

I was at a party recently where I was introduced to a friend-of-a-friend. Within the first five minutes of our conversation, he had told me about his old business, his new business, everyone he knew who was remotely related to my business, and how much money he lost when he sold his last house. Now this was a friendly, outgoing guy who was just making conversation at a party. But the things he communicated and the way he communicated them told me a great deal about who he was and what he considered important.

I taught a couples' Bible study for several years, and was continually amazed at some of the things guys would say about their wives or families in public. Usually the couple would be sitting side by side, so I could watch the wife's posture stiffen and face redden while her unguarded husband spilled the family beans, oblivious to the trouble he was brewing. As soon as I could, I'd always interject and try to move us back into safer water, but often the damage was already done. And you could always tell how severe the aftermath had been, because it was usually several weeks before that husband would open his mouth in the group again.

When we open our mouths, we're opening the front drapes to our souls. We're sending out for public consumption the thoughts, feelings, and attitudes that rule our inner lives, and once free they can go a long way toward ruling our outer lives as well. At our house, we always try to make sure the house is straightened up and presentable before we open the front drapes. Sometimes that means we don't open them when we'd like, and sometimes it means we don't open them at all. Our mouths could probably learn a thing or two from our drapes.

The day did finally come when Beth told me she loved me. Yet over the years that I've teased her about her "thank you" in the chapel, she's firmly defended the validity of her response. Like me, she knew the significance of saying "I love you," and she simply wasn't sure yet. At the time, every fiber of my being wished she would do the expedient, comfortable, diplomatic thing and say, "I love you too." She could always recant later, right? That's what I had done with those words in the past. But now, having heard those words sincerely from her for a few years, I know how much more precious they are when they're more than just words.

Of the nine "arenas" where a guy displays his character, communication now begins a new "trilogy" of arenas that go beyond a guy's independent, mostly autonomous life. The character and maturity we demonstrate in the first three arenas of discipline—decisions, work, and play—may or may not affect other people. But in communication, we are by definition touching others, pulling them into this dynamic arena with us. Sometimes that communication "touch" is very deep, and can bring with it great pleasure or great pain.

The issue isn't how much or how loud or even how well we communicate. Those things will vary depending on our individual personalities and talents. The important question is: when we do choose to communicate, how do we go about it? The boy in us heartily endorses Beth's "thank you" response, because the boy in us always communicates with truthfulness.

"NO KIDDING!"

The boy in us communicates with truthfulness

"Always tell the truth." It's a platitude coached into us from our earliest days of cognizance. Little George Washington chopped down a cherry tree, told the truth about it, and became President. Abraham Lincoln was overpaid a few pennies, walked a couple of miles to settle the account, and became President. The implication? If I just tell the truth, I can become President, even with a criminal juvenile record and no apparent mathematical skills.

Though truthfulness is often touted as an uncommon virtue, the fact is that we're all born with a natural unguardedness, a bent toward telling the truth. This by no means implies that we're anything but sinful and self-seeking creatures from conception. But it does seem to take a few years before we learn to effectively conceal our various delinquencies with deceitful communication.

The boy in us reminds us how noble and uncomplicated it is to simply tell the truth. Sure there are nuances or euphemisms or politically correct terminology that might make communication smoother, but the boy in us sees all those as wasting time or lacking integrity. Just tell the truth, he urges us, and let the chips fall where they may. It worked for George and Abe, didn't it?

A Few Pennies for Your Thoughts

My three-year-old son, Noah, was standing in the middle of the living room floor when I came around the corner. He wasn't doing anything—yet—just standing there. He looked up at me and said, "Daddy, I want you to leave." Actually I was planning on just passing through, but his insistence on my departure intrigued me.

"Why do you want me to leave? I just got here." I baited him.

"I don't want you to see what I'm going to do," he replied with an incredible mixture of truthfulness and mischievousness.

"What are you going to do?" I wouldn't have left the room now for anything.

"Dump out the pennies."

"The pennies" were in a huge glass jar with a cork in the top. We occasionally had let the boys get a few out and play with them in little measuring cups, thinking it might encourage them toward careers in banking or high finance. But we had always denied their requests to dump the entire jar out on the floor, and they knew they weren't to get the pennies out without Mommy's or Daddy's supervision.

"No, you know you're not supposed to do that," I countered, trying not to smile as I reconfirmed the law of the land.

"I know," he sighed, and walked away to find something else to do. Then it was my turn to walk away, shuddering as I imagined the day when his communication could better conceal his true thoughts and motives.

Kids Say the Darnedest Things

While my younger son keeps us amused with his unguarded, truthful statements, our older son has started to humble and occasionally bewilder us with his truthful questions. As we walked out of a funeral home visitation one afternoon, we could tell Caleb was deep in thought. We had decided it was wise to acquaint our kids with death and teach them about its realities, so the funeral home seemed like a good idea. But Caleb's serious expression was making us wonder if the experience had been too traumatic.

"Caleb, is something wrong?" his mother asked softly.

"No." Her question brought his thoughts back from the grave and he was ready with his question. "I was just wondering, did that man have legs when he was alive?"

It would never have occurred to us to explain that the half-open coffin was concealing the man's legs, but Caleb had never seen a person lying in a box before. With his limited understanding, he was both seeking and expressing what appeared to be the simple truth of the matter—dead people don't have legs. Once we convinced him they didn't "saw you in half" when you die, he was fine.

The Truth, the Whole Truth, and Nothing but the Truth

The boy in us always tells it like it is, or at least how he perceives that it is. He asks questions with that same refreshing candor. When the boy in us governs our communication there are no fronts, facades, or euphemisms. He would make an excellent journalist. He would make a poor political "spin doctor."

The boy in us is completely trusting and vulnerable in what he says, and he expects others to be equally forthright. He makes deals with handshakes rather than contracts. He says "yummy" when he likes something and "yuck" when he doesn't. His yes means yes, and his no means no.

The boy in us is interested in describing things as they really are, not as someone else would like them to be. He's interested in asking questions that get to the point. In fact, he uses truth-seeking questions like the military uses heat-seeking missiles, and he won't be sidetracked or hoodwinked with patronizing answers or other evasive maneuvers.

Truth and Consequences

In communication, as in so many other arenas, the boy in us gives us courage and boldness. He not only holds the truth in highest esteem, he's troubled when anything less than unadulterated truth seems to be prevailing. So when he sees someone being cheated by "the system," he speaks up. When he sees someone trying to cheat the system themselves, he speaks up too. The boy in us isn't on the side of anyone in particular, he's on the side of the truth.

Of course, not being on anyone's side can be a very lonely place to stand. Unadulterated truth is actually a rare commodity, and standing for what's true is almost certain to make more enemies than friends. When the boy in us is strongly in control of our communication, he makes us a sort of "prophet." Did you ever hear of a happy-go-lucky, carefree prophet? No, prophets have always been loners who often live hard lives with a pretty stern view of their situation. The reason they can live with hardship and that stern view is that they also live with a surpassingly stronger view of the truth and its ultimate victory.

In the meantime, our prophetic days can be tough ones. Set apart from expedient alliances that would compromise our standard of truth, we can find ourselves isolated and vulnerable. People don't always want to hear the truth, and so speaking it involves certain risks. At best, a prophet may be alienated, or poor. At worst, he may be fired, or beheaded.

Still, the boy in us can give us the courage we need to be a prophet, even when the consequences are undesirable. He tells us to boldly speak the truth, and to bank on the ultimate victory. In the workplace, at home, in the marketplace, at church—he helps us say what's true and right, rather than just what's comfortable.

The Judgmental Brat in Us

"Do you have a hobby?"

The question caught me by surprise. I was on my way out of the junior high locker room, my hair still wet from the shower and my knees still floor-burned from the tough game we had just narrowly lost. Our eighth-grade basketball team had now dropped three games in a row, all by five points or less.

"A hobby?!" I repeated. "What do you mean?"

I looked up to see that the question was coming from the older brother of one of my teammates. Fred was the center on our team, the leading scorer and generally the best player. His brother was three or four years older than us, and I didn't remember him ever talking to me before. But I was impressed with his personal interest in me now, and was glad to get my mind off the disappointing game.

"You know, a hobby," he repeated. "Something you like to do with your time."

"Well actually I've just started collecting coins," I offered. "It's funny you should ask, my uncle was just showing me how . . ." Fred's brother didn't let me finish.

"I KNOW what your hobby is. I've seen you do it three times now. It's losing basketball games!"

Suddenly I was yanked out of my non-threatening coin collection and back into reliving the heated battle we had just lost. Fred's brother didn't care about my hobby. His question was just setting up a cruel, satirical criticism of my play. My defense mechanisms rallied and I searched for a comeback to his humiliating jest. But I had no reply for him. During the closing seconds of the game I had tried to get the ball to Fred. But in my haste I had lost control of my dribble and kicked the ball out-of-bounds. My mistake was the most visible reason for our defeat. His criticism was mean, but true. And I've never forgotten his words.

The Truth Hurts

Truthfulness can be a very hurtful thing, often more so than lies. When someone hurts you with a lie, there's a good chance the lie can be refuted or proven over time to be untrue and the harm diminished. But when someone hurts you with the truth, the hurt usually sticks.

Knowing how powerful the truth can be, the brat in us chooses to use it as a weapon of destruction rather than a tool of reconciliation. Because he is essentially selfish, the brat in us uses what he knows to be true to get what he wants from others. Blackmail and extortion are destructive uses of the truth, yet these mafiaesque crimes are far less prevalent and no more abusive than the way Christians can use even biblical truth to coerce, manipulate, or just plain bully one another.

Hurtful communication—trash talking, if you will—is meant to tear down rather than build up. We guys are especially susceptible to it because we're continually placing ourselves in such competitive positions and roles. It's become almost accepted etiquette to taunt, goad, and provoke your competition or adversary in hopes of intimidating him. In fact, such verbal abuse has even become common between coaches and players, and between teammates. Trash talking is supposed to be motivational. It's supposed to get your juices flowing. The problem lies in how deeply you have to cut to find those juices, and how permanent the scars are once the game is over.

Balancing the Boy

At his best, the boy in us brings honesty and integrity to communication. He speaks the truth and demands it of others. He exposes ulterior motives.

At his worst, the brat in us uses truth without regard to its effect on others. The truth is too powerful a weapon to be used selfishly or carelessly. That's why truthfulness in communication needs to be tempered with compassion for those affected, and compassion is what helps the man in us to communicate with tact.

"YOU DON'T SAY"

The man in us communicates with tact

While the boy in us never hesitates to tell the truth, the man in us has endured truth's consequences enough to develop a slightly different approach. He's learned when it pays to be tactful. The man in us is usually the diplomat who can appreciate a delicate situation and choose an appropriately delicate response.

Let's face it, there are some questions whose truthful answers serve no constructive purpose. Questions like: Do you like my hair? How's the meatloaf? How much do you think I weigh now? What was that word Grandpa said when he stubbed his toe? Do you think I used too much salt? Isn't this the cutest baby you've ever seen? Inevitably those questions are followed by an insistent, *"Tell me the truth, now."*

One of my favorites is the one that comes at the other end of an early Saturday morning phone call: "I didn't wake you up did I?" Now what's the point in answering a question like that truthfully? The harm's been done, the damage irreversible, and I'm supposed to make it worse by milking a guilt-ridden apology out of the transgressor? No, I avoid lying if possible and instead come up with some tactful or evasive reply like, "What, are you kidding?" or, "Do you think I sleep this late?"

The key to avoiding the truth without lying is in answering a question with another question. That's not wrong is it? Tell me the truth, now.

Just Passing By

Dating requires a lot more tact than marriage. After you're married for a while, you find there's very little you wouldn't say to your partner. But when you're dating, you sometimes find there are all kinds of things you can't say yet.

I wasn't yet at the "say anything" stage with Beth when we dated our way into a delicate situation. We were driving in my car on our way to a party at a friend's house. About halfway there, I suddenly noticed a foul odor. We were in a residential neighborhood, not out in the country, so I knew the odor was probably human. I also knew that I had not produced it—we guys can also control our noises and smells a lot better before we're married, I've noticed. That only left Beth.

I was surprised and a little disgusted. I had never in my life known any girl who would allow that to happen in an enclosed car, and especially not on a date. But then my disbelief and annoyance turned to concern. *She must be sick!* I thought. *This is the classiest, most beautiful girl I've ever known. She would never do something like this if she could control it! Maybe I should ask her if she's feeling okay. Maybe I should offer to take her home. Maybe I should crack a window.*

By the time all those thoughts had passed through my head, the odor seemed to have passed through my car. I decided the tactful thing to say was absolutely nothing, at least for now. She was probably sitting there feeling embarrassed, and anything I could say would only heighten her humiliation. If it happened again, maybe I'd just take her to the hospital.

I tried to put the awkward situation out of my mind, and we went on to enjoy the party. I had almost forgotten the incident when, on the way home, she did it again. I couldn't believe it. This relationship had to be reevaluated, I thought. I turned my head away from her to catch a breath, and noticed that we were at the exact same spot as before. Then it hit me.

"Did you know there's a sewage treatment plant down at the bottom of that hill?" I asked matter-of-factly. "I'd hate to live around here, because when the wind is just right—or rather just wrong—you can smell it for blocks."

There, that's safe, I thought. *If it is her, she has an excuse now. If it's not her, I may be able to let her in my car again.*

Tremendous relief seemed to sweep over Beth's face, and she exclaimed, "Oh is THAT what it is! I thought it was you!"

It then occurred to me that she had been thinking the same repulsive thoughts about me that I had been thinking about her. As we laughed hysterically at each other's hidden thoughts, our communication opened up to other unspoken misconceptions we had of each other. From that moment on, our relationship entered a new level of intimacy. We found that once you've talked about human odors, you can talk about almost anything.

The Tactical Tactics of Tact

It's no accident that the words "tactical" and "tactic" both begin with tact. Tact is what lets you restrain your communication for some strategic reason. You don't say what you normally would, because you desire a different outcome than the blatant, outspoken truth would probably produce. Often that outcome has to do with who the person you're speaking to is and how they would receive the undiluted truth. The boy in us doesn't usually think that far ahead in his communication, and the brat in us simply doesn't care how others might respond. In both cases the message being sent is given a higher value than the receiver of the message.

But the man in us is very aware of the receiver. He reminds us that there are lots of different ways to communicate the same message, and that making sure you play your message to the personality and needs of your listener can make your communication much more effective. When the boy in us says, "Who cares? Just tell the truth!" the man in us quickly replies, "I care! The truth can be 'packaged' and still be the uncompromising truth." The man in us recognizes that packaged truth sometimes lands on more receptive ears than raw truth. And because he wants communication, not just proclamation, because he wants results, not just integrity, he chooses his words very carefully.

The same man in us who is principle-driven in his decisions and cautious in his personal disciplines is the one who helps us be tactful in our communication. He's the part of us that remembers the insensitive or hurtful things we've said in the past, and helps us think a little further ahead this time.

The Cowardly Jerk in Us

There's a big difference between strategically restraining your words because you want to affect a positive outcome and repressing the truth because you're afraid of the consequences. The jerk in us is the part of us that chooses the apparent safety of non-communication over the inherent risks of honest communication.

The more we yield to the cowardly jerk in us, the more others will take advantage of us. They know we'll offer no resistance, so they push us as far as they can. The cowardly jerk in us invites our boss to be a tyrant, our wife to be a nag, and our children to be disrespectful and disobedient. In effect, he says those things are okay, because they're better than confrontation. The cowardly jerk in us hates confrontation.

Double-Dating in Dad's Car

I didn't know Jeanie very well on our first date, and she didn't know me very well either. We basically approved of each other's appearance, but the real occasion for our being together was the other half of our double date—Jack and Rhonda. As I recall, Rhonda wanted to find a date for her friend and Jack wanted to find a chauffeur for his date. We drove my dad's new car.

It was a frigid winter evening, with temperatures well below zero. After the movie, we piled into the car and let it warm up for a minute while we talked about where to go for pizza. Then Jeanie dropped the bombshell.

"Do you mind if I smoke?"

Her cigarettes were already in her hand, and she was putting one to her lips while my mouth was still wide open. All I could think of was what my dad would say if he knew I let someone smoke in his new car. I give Jack credit though, he recovered first.

"No, you'd better not," he replied tentatively but courageously. "This is his dad's new car and everything . . ."

From the disbelieving looks on both Jeanie's and Rhonda's faces, I could tell Jack was crawling out on a limb, the lonely limb of not being cool. Both girls told him to lighten up, and reminded him it wasn't his car. It would just be one cigarette, and they assured him the car wouldn't smell as long as the window was cracked. They then turned to me for the final verdict, and I had to decide whether or not to crawl out on the uncool limb with Jack. I decided instead to abruptly saw him off.

"Oh, it will be all right." I was trying to convince myself at the same time. "Lighten up, Jack."

I could tell Jack was a little disappointed in me, but he didn't say so. Having stood unsuccessfully for the truth of my dad's convictions, Jack now chose to stand for his own.

"Well, smoke really bothers me, and I'd rather you didn't."

Though I had already cast my cowardly lot, inside I desperately hoped Jack would prevail. My dad would kill me if he knew I let someone smoke in his new car.

Jack didn't prevail. And so in my one and only date with her, Jeanie proceeded to fill my dad's new car with smoke. Once she lit up, she decided it was too cold to crack the window. My friend Jack had chosen to speak with courageous truth, while I chose to speak with cowardly tact. I thought about the difference a lot that winter night, especially after I dropped them all off early and drove around for two hours in sub-zero temperatures—with all the windows down.

Balancing the Man

The tactful man in us helps us communicate with an end result in mind. Often he can help us avoid hurting others unnecessarily with our words. With tact governing our communication, we can help or lead others without alienating them. We can share our ideas, opinions, and values without making others feel theirs are being threatened. We can say what's true and still be encouraging.

But we can't compromise truth to avoid confrontation. We can't go silently along with whatever is being said or done just to avoid the consequences of speaking for what's right. It's possible to communicate with both integrity and effectiveness, to say what's true with encouragement too. But to communicate with that delicate balance between truth and tact requires that our words be governed with a special attitude—the attitude of love.

SAYING WHAT'S TRUE

With Encouragement Too

LOVE in Communication:
Truthfulness and Tact in the Balance

Probably the most important question to ask in measuring effective communication is, "Does it get through?" A guy who's striving for maturity in his character wants the way he communicates with others to be more than impressive, or persuasive, or charming, or even "right." When we express ourselves—whether it's to family, friends, acquaintances, or strangers—we should want a clear, unhindered representation of what's inside us. And equally important, we should want that message to find its mark. It's not enough to be eloquent or witty or wise, or even correct. We should want to be understood. If our message doesn't "get through," our communication is incomplete.

Both the truthful boy in us and the tactful man in us can contribute to this kind of communication. A guy who communicates truthfully shows that he has integrity. You can believe what he says. You can take him at face value. You can trust him. And people listen to those they trust.

At the same time, a guy who communicates tactfully shows that he has compassion. More than just caring about what's true or right, he cares about how what's true or right affects people. Even when he has to say hard things, you know it's not just to be hurtful or manipulative. He cares about you. And people listen to those who care about them.

110

Integrity devoid of compassion can produce words that are sharp, judgmental, and often destructive. And compassion devoid of integrity can produce words that are merely superficial and expedient. In the long run, those can be just as destructive. The mature balance between truthfulness and tactfulness is to communicate with love—to say what's true, but with encouragement too.

True Friends

There certainly are light or amusing illustrations of loving communication. For example, there was the time a lady approached my preacher father just before the morning service to tell him he had a little green "friend" on the end of his nose. She didn't want him to deliver the morning message in that condition, and though it embarrassed her terribly to be so bold about his "companion," she knew he'd want to know. She definitely told him the truth, and one could hardly imagine more tactful terms than "friend" and "companion." In other words, the communication she offered him that morning—and the tissue—were certainly delivered with love.

The truth is, however, that most genuinely loving communication is neither light nor amusing. More often it's heart-wrenching and costly. Sometimes it's sacrificial.

As I mentioned earlier, I spent most of my first year in college in spiritual rebellion and struggle. When God mercifully drew me back to himself, I transferred to a new college. At the old college, I left behind a very good friend, one who had only known me during perhaps the most wayward year of my Christian life. Over the next three or four years of spiritual re-rooting, I kept in contact with Brett. After we each graduated, I went to visit him for a weekend.

As we traded notes on our lives, I found myself deeply needing to communicate to Brett what had happened in my life spiritually. Though he had occasionally attended church with me the year we were in school together, it became evident as we talked that relationship with a personal God was not something he had yet experienced. At one point, he pierced my heart with the statement that I was the only "real Christian" he had ever known.

Recalling his statement still makes my eyes well up with tears.

I remember praying silently at the time, *"Oh, God, forgive me. He's saying the worst year of my Christian life was the best look he's had at faith in You!"* A sense of responsibility overwhelmed me. I had one weekend to try and communicate the truth about the Christian life. Yet I knew Brett well enough to know he wouldn't be pushed.

The last night we were together, we spent four or five hours over a pizza. Once again he listened politely to the account of my new life, but I could tell it remained only my experience in his heart. My communication intensified. Our time together was fading away, and I wasn't getting through. I grew bolder and bolder with my statements, then backed off as I saw him bristle. I tried softening the message, hardening it, repackaging it, then letting it rest for a while.

Only a couple of other times in my life have I communicated with such love. Once was when a good friend's marriage was coming apart. The other was when my own marriage was finally coming together. Each time required risky, confrontational, and ultimately sacrificial words. Each time was emotionally and spiritually exhausting.

I was also exhausted by the time Brett drove me to the airport. Our parting words had to do with my experience being real for me but not for him. At least not yet.

I continue to write the truth to Brett, and I continue to pray for him. I'm also tactful in my communication—Brett is not his real name. Why can't I stop communicating to him and about him? I guess I still love him.

Love-Driven Communication

Love is the soft coating in which hard truth is most effectively communicated. At the same time, love can give great power to even the most tactful message. Love can motivate you to say things easier left unsaid, yet allow you to read the receptivity and emotions of your listener, and back off if necessary.

You can tell an awful lot about a guy's character by how he communicates. Does he yell at his kids, or does he discipline them? Does he "schmooze" his clients, or does he help them? Does he flatter his co-workers, or does he praise them? Does he hold things back from his wife, or does he open up his soul to her?

The difference in all those contrasts is primarily one of attitude toward the person with whom you are communicating. It's not a matter of how much you communicate, or even how well. If your attitude is one of genuine love, respect or concern, it will come through in how you talk to them. If your attitude toward someone is indifferent or selfish, nothing you say will be able to compensate for what was missing before you opened your mouth.

It takes time and deliberate effort to make both the substance and style of our communication truly loving. Sometimes it means holding back our words for the right time or the right mood. Sometimes it means saying hard things now, while the moment is ripe. It rarely means saying whatever is on the tip of our tongue. Like all acts of love, loving communication is at its best when things like forethought, planning, mood-setting, relaxation, and tenderness govern each word.

When my wife and I need some quality talk-time, we play Ping-Pong in our basement. It relaxes us, keeps us alert (as opposed to when we try to talk at bedtime) and gives whatever we're talking about an atmosphere of fun. With friends, I've had great communication over a can of pop or while shooting baskets in the driveway. With others, the telephone seems to work best. In all cases, there's something about taking the time to plan and stage a fun or non-threatening atmosphere that lets us know we love each other, whatever might need to be said.

Jesus and Communication

When "the rich young ruler" came to Jesus asking about eternal life, Mark records that Jesus looked at him and loved him. The natural product of that love was that Jesus told him the truth about himself. The young man was allowing his wealth to hinder his relationship to God.

When a woman caught in adultery was brought to Jesus, there were already plenty of people hurling the truth at her, soon to be followed by stones. Jesus tactfully turned the truth back on the bratty, judgmental mob, then turned to speak softly of forgiveness and redemption to a woman whom the truth had almost killed.

At first glance, love seems more like a character trait that should describe the next arena—relationships—rather than communication. And relationships are certainly an appropriate place to talk about love. But Jesus shows us by His very existence that the ultimate expression, the ultimate communication of God's love was in sending His living Word to become flesh and dwell among us. Love, by nature, chooses to communicate Jesus' life, but even more so His death and resurrection prove that God's standard for communication is both penetrating truth and encouraging redemption, both from a heart of love. Such communication, of course, takes place in the context of the next character arena—the arena of relationships.

Don't Just Take My Word for It

Communicating like a truthful boy can be good:

Lord, who may enter your Temple? Who may worship on Zion, your sacred hill? A person who obeys God in everything and always does what is right, whose words are true and sincere, and who does not slander others. He does no wrong to his friends nor spreads rumors about his neighbors. (Psalm 15:1–3)

———

Communicating like a judgmental brat is bad:

Do not judge others, so that God will not judge you, for God will judge you in the same way you judge others, and he will apply to you the same rules you apply to others. (Matthew 7:1–2)

———

Communicating like a tactful man can be good:

A gentle answer quiets anger, but a harsh one stirs it up. . . . Kind words bring life, but cruel words crush your spirit. (Proverbs 15:1, 4)

———

Communicating like a cowardly jerk is bad:

> *Better to correct someone openly than to let him think you don't care for him at all.* (Proverbs 27:5)

―――――――

Loving communication is that which balances truthfulness and tactfulness:

> *Instead, by speaking the truth in a spirit of love, we must grow up in every way to Christ, who is the head.* (Ephesians 4:15)

> *I may be able to speak the languages of men and even of angels, but if I have no love, my speech is no more than a noisy gong or a clanging bell.* (1 Corinthians 13:1)

Character Trait #5
Humility
in Relationships

...seeking good
for ANOTHER
without trying
to SMOTHER

SHE LOVES ME, SHE LOVES ME NOT

There comes a time in each guy's life when he basically changes his mind about girls. Up until that time, girls are scum-of-the-earth sissies with no redeeming qualities whatsoever. In short, they are icky. But after the change of mind (some would argue the loss of mind) takes place, no mountain is too high, no battle too dangerous, no shopping mall too vast or boring to separate us from the woman we love.

I'm sure there are certain biological, sociological, and psychological reasons that determine when this change of mind about girls takes place. All I know is it's usually sometime before a guy starts shaving and after he stops wearing underwear with cartoon characters on them. Often it centers around one special girl who will forever bear the honor of being "the first." For me, that time was sixth grade and that girl was Pam.

Living for Smiles

I was smitten with Pam a long time before I had the courage to do anything about it. Our alphabetical seating in class placed me in the front of the first row. Pam was about halfway back in one of the middle rows. Two times each morning and two times each afternoon, I'd allow myself to steal a glance at Pam over my left shoulder. Sometimes she'd notice me and sometimes she wouldn't. When she didn't notice me, the disappointment would literally make my stomach hurt. When she did notice me, her eyes would sparkle and she'd flash her terrific smile at me in a way that was shy and bewitching at the same time. Quickly, I'd turn back to my work before my blushing cheeks could fully redden and give me away. But whatever schoolwork I should have been working on at the time received no real attention for the next several minutes.

The Plot Thickens

If it were up to me, Pam and I could have continued like that forever, but sixth-grade society was progressing around me, and my friends soon informed me that I needed to give expression to my affection for Pam. How? My best friend would tell Pam's best friend to tell Pam that I liked her. If she responded that she liked me, we were officially "going together." If she responded that she didn't like me, my best friend and I would insist that the whole thing was a misunderstanding, and that I had really said I liked Spam, not Pam. Okay, sixth-grade society wasn't progressing that much.

The lunch hour when I waited for Pam's response, my stomach hurt more than all the times she hadn't looked at me combined. When the reply came that she liked me too, however, I managed to receive the news with all the I-knew-it-all-the-time grace and humility that usually characterize sixth-grade boys. Pam and I were "going together." I could hardly wait to see if that meant we would someday exchange words.

No, my friends informed me that the next step was to continue performing daily check-ups to ascertain whether Pam still liked me or not. Things like this can change at a moment's notice, they said, and you need to keep asking. The average sixth-grade romance is measured in hours, not days or weeks.

I couldn't help but wonder if my best friend didn't just like talking to Pam's best friend, but I went along with protocol. After all, the suspense and melodrama of finding out whether love had survived another day was kind of exciting, especially when the ego-boosting assurance was usually that it had. Day after day, we played the he-likes-you-do-you-still-like-him game, and day after day the reassuring "yes" came back from her to her to him to me.

The Ultimatum

Like I said, if it were up to me, we could have continued our relationship just like that right on up through marriage. That's why I was so shocked when one day Pam's reply deviated from the script. I was sitting there waiting for my regular "yes" and feeling pretty smug when I noticed the worried expression on my approaching friend's face. Something was amuck.

"Well?" I asked impatiently, my heart beating faster than it had since that first ego-on-the-line day. I suddenly realized that it was too late in the game to still use the Spam line.

"She still likes you, but . . ."

But? BUT??! I didn't let him finish his sentence. Her "but" was stuck in my throat and I tried desperately to dislodge it, to make it go away by repeating it over and over in disbelief. But what?

" . . . but she says you'd better do something about it."

"Like what?" was of course my panicked follow-up question. But my friend didn't know the answer. He wasn't used to any answer but "yes" either. Suddenly we were in over our heads. I didn't know how to respond. I needed some help. I needed some insight. I needed some counsel. I needed to go to the bathroom.

The bathroom, of course, is the conference room where sixth-grade guys can pool their collective wisdom about girls and what makes them tick. Unfortunately, the collective wisdom sixth-grade guys have about girls could fit neatly on one of the bathroom tiles, and that day the graffiti artists of old were of no help whatsoever. We had to send my friend back into the lioness den for a clue.

When he returned from his mission, he was ready to shed light on our ignorance. Pam wanted a ring, or an ID bracelet—something to show that she was my girl friend. She might as well have asked me for a do-it-yourself blood transfusion on the teacher's desk, because I owned nothing remotely resembling a ring or ID bracelet.

Pam's ultimatum practically blew the doors off the stalls in the boys' conference room. None of us guys had ever played in that league of relationship before. When you got into giving rings or bracelets, well, you were practically making your relationship public for adults and parents and everybody! Pam was asking me to do more than follow the norms of sixth-grade relationships—she was asking me to set the pace with her. And at that moment I wanted to set the pace by punching the teeth out of her winsome smile, and blackening both of her sparkling eyes.

The Rewards and Risks of Relationships

I won't recount here all I had to go through in order to acquire an acceptable ring for Pam, or how I explained to my parents its immediate disappearance. Suffice it to say that Pam made me earn those cute smiles and "yes" answers the hard way. In the days and weeks that followed, Pam would lead me through hand-holding, book-carrying, and behind-the-bleachers kissing. Each brave new step introduced me to the risks and the rewards that go with bona fide two-way relationships.

You see, before Pam, my relationships had been much simpler and more pragmatic. I related to my parents because I needed them. My parents told me what to do because they were responsible for me and knew what was best for me. My friends were guys who were interested in the same activities or sports as I was. In all cases, my relationships were pretty incidental to the task at hand. They were something you found along the road, not a destination in and of themselves. In a way, Pam was my first live destination.

It's still pretty common, maybe even natural, for guys to approach relationships that way. We have an end in mind—a job, a hobby, sports, sex, money, power, religion—and we find relationships to be helpful means to those ends. But in the process, hopefully, we discover what marvelous ends relationships are in themselves. We find that friendships can be better than jobs or hobbies, marriage can be better than sex, partnerships can be better than money, mentoring can be better than power, and discipleship can be better than religion. We find people to be eternal beings with eternal qualities, and we find they can satisfy our souls in ways that things or tasks can't.

The Pams in our lives show us, sometimes painfully, the value and the cost of engaging a smile and taking it to the next step, of expressing an emotion and letting it lead to a commitment. The more significant give-and-take relationships we experience, the more we realize that our "on the way" relationships can be far more significant than the destinations we thought were so important. Usually it's the boy in us that leads the way into those relationships, because the boy in us recognizes how much pleasure and fulfillment is to be found in others, in relationships.

"WANNA MAKE OUT?"

The boy in us takes pleasure from others

The basic problem we find in relating to people is that they don't always do what we want. In fact, many people have this nasty habit of expecting us to do what they want instead. A friend of mine has a great phrase he uses when he finds himself in disagreement or conflict with someone. He simply says, "I'm not experiencing you the way I want to experience you." It's a great line to use with pushy salesmen, obnoxiously undisciplined children, or attitude-impaired waitresses.

The boy in us recognizes how true my friend's tongue-in-cheek expression really is. In each relationship we undertake, we desire to experience the other person in a particular way—a way that brings us satisfaction and pleasure. That's the main reason the boy in us relates at all! He likes people. He knows they can be fun, or stimulating, or helpful, or interesting. He appreciates their talents, their appearance, their ideas, their power—and he wants to enjoy them. The boy in us knows how to take pleasure in his relationships.

Smooching in the Stairwell

It was my birthday. I don't really remember which one—probably my fifteenth or sixteenth—life was going by with such speed and confusion during those teenage years. What I remember vividly is the present Shelly gave me.

Shelly was one of the girls in my church youth group. We had never dated each other before, but we had flirted a little. Shelly's family lived far from the church. In fact, she attended a different

122

high school and had a different set of friends. Church was the only time we really saw each other.

In the days leading up to my birthday, our mutual flirting had seemed to intensify. A playful comment here, a teasing look there, an occasional lingering touch—all let me (and my hormones) know that something exploratory was going on between us. When the youth group piled into a car to go for pizza, I started making a deliberate effort to make sure Shelly and I piled in next to each other. There's nothing like a big youth group "smoosh" in the backseat of a car to help two semi-coy teenagers get better acquainted.

Then Shelly had started talking about the "present" she wanted to give me for my birthday. Now the mere word "present" can't begin to do justice to what Shelly was promising me, or the way in which she was promising it. The playful glimmer in her eye, the knowing smile on her lips, the casual flick of her hair—yes, the promise of the present was much more exciting than the word itself. By the time my birthday rolled around, my pulse would race when she walked into the room. Long before Shelly actually delivered my present, I had "shaken it" many times in my thoughts.

Thank goodness my birthday was on a Sunday that year. When the youth group returned to the church from its Sunday night activity, several kids usually hung around at the church waiting for their parents to pick them up. My house (I was the pastor's son) was next door to the church and Shelly had driven herself, so we both could have gone straight home from the parking lot. Instead, we both went back inside the church. I personally was about to overdose on anticipation. Shelly too seemed a little nervous as she wished me happy birthday and asked me if I was ready for my present. Boy, was I ready for my present.

Because there were still kids and youth leaders hanging around the church, and because those youth leaders would eventually be concerned if Shelly's car was there and Shelly wasn't, we only had a few minutes to look for some privacy. Stealing away from the group, we found ourselves in a back stairwell that was rarely used. For the next fifteen minutes or so, we stood there whispering, giggling, embracing, kissing, and then kissing some more. It was a wonderful, wonderful birthday present.

No Strings Attached

I'm not sure whether any mature, self-respecting female can read the above account without clucking her tongue and shaking her head in disapproval. "There are names for girls like that!" I can almost hear the accusing tone. "Teenage guys just have one thing on their mind. In fact, ALL guys . . ." Fortunately, since I'm doing the writing here, I can cut the criticism off there, at least for now. Guys will understand better, at least those viewing this scene through the eyes of the boy in us.

I guess Shelly and I were gratifying our desires and attraction to each other outside the commitment of a serious relationship. Some might characterize our kissing encounter as borderline promiscuous. Unchecked, it might have led us into more dangerous waters.

The truth is, as much as we both enjoyed it, that one encounter in the stairwell was the only time Shelly and I ever kissed. She was a couple of years older than I, and just starting into a dating relationship with someone at her school. I wasn't dating anyone at the time, but didn't feel that dating Shelly seriously was very practical or desirable.

For a few days leading up to my birthday, and for fifteen very special minutes on the day of my birthday, Shelly and I just purely enjoyed each other. There were no strings attached, no expectations, no commitment, no follow-up required. That's the way the boy in us loves to approach our relationships. He looks at others in the context of the enjoyment or pleasure they can bring to his life. He appreciates what others can do for him or how they can make him feel.

This desire to enjoy others isn't limited to guy-girl relationships. I can remember wanting my dad to go out in the yard and pitch a baseball with me. I had no concept of what his responsibilities were or what he would have to set aside in order to give me that time. I just wanted him to come play. I wanted to enjoy him for the fun he could bring me.

I remember visiting my college roommate and his wife a few years after we were both married. Long after our spouses went to bed, Greg and I stayed up in his living room into the wee hours of the morning, laughing, reminiscing, looking at yearbooks, just enjoying each other for who we were and what we liked in each other. That guy can make me belly-laugh more than anyone I know, and when I get to be with him, I just want to indulge myself. Greg simply makes me feel great.

Parents and grandparents can do the same thing. How many Little League games have you seen where a zealous father is clearly after his own enjoyment rather than his son's? How many grandmothers have you seen who insist on planting a big, wet, lipstick kiss on a ten-year-old's cheek when they know he'd rather drink asparagus juice? All kinds of relationships can be approached in all kinds of ways with the same basic premise—*"I want to enjoy you!"*

Replenishing Friends

As Beth and I were leaving the house of some good friends one night, one of them made the comment, "We need to find more time to spend with you."

Her comment seemed unusually phrased, but I responded by rephrasing what I thought her sentiment to be. "Yes, we really enjoyed tonight too. We'll have to do this more often." But I hadn't understood the significance of what she was saying.

"No, I mean we NEED to spend some more time with you. You two are among our few replenishing friends."

She then proceeded to tell us of some reading she had done that described the different types of friendships people have. So many friendships are unilateral, where one person or one couple is attempting to meet the needs of another. Those relationships benefit one side of the friendship, but are often a drain on the other side. Our good friends were expressing what we too felt about our relationship, that it was one of those relatively rare ones where both sides benefit and are emotionally replenished. We could genuinely enjoy each other without being preoccupied with each other's needs or demands. The boy in us loves relationships like that.

The Self-Gratifying Brat in Us

When I was in eighth grade, a seventh-grade girl named Vicki "liked" me. She had one of her friends tell one of my friends to tell me so (see earlier story about Pam if you've forgotten exactly how this works). I didn't particularly "like" Vicki, so I promptly and courteously returned my rejection notice through the proper channels.

The next day, I happened to be with my friend Dennis when another of Vicki's friends approached him and told him Vicki now liked him. Apparently she didn't want to use the same friend on her second (third? fifth?) choice, and this friend of hers didn't know I had been previously solicited. When Dennis was presented with Vicki's proposal, he was obviously interested. Unfortunately, that's when the brat in me kicked in. I didn't value Vicki's affection, but I was a little put off at how quickly she had dismissed her need for mine and moved on to plan B. I decided to enjoy some mean, bratty self-gratification at Vicki's expense.

I took Dennis aside and told him I had received the same proposition the day before. He agreed to be a brat with me and "test" Vicki's affection for him. We sent word back that Dennis liked Vicki, then sent word through a different girl that I had changed my mind and liked her too. When Vicki sent her "cancellation notice" back to Dennis, we were ready for her. We promptly sent word back that neither one of us really liked her. I remember feeling a little bad when I heard that the news made her cry.

I don't recount that story because I'm proud of it. It just illustrates how approaching relationships solely for the pleasure or enjoyment they can bring can quickly deteriorate into using people as objects of self-gratification. While the boy in us may be less than fully considerate of other people in a relationship or unaware of how they are affected by his behavior, the brat in us deliberately disregards the other person's well-being. The brat in us, in effect, says, "You're here to please me, and my main interest in you is what I can get from you."

My smooching with Shelly may illustrate the uncomplicated bliss of a low-maintenance, fun-filled relationship, but it's not a long jump from that line of thinking into a rationale for legalized prostitution or any number of other if-it-feels-good-do-it vices. In reality, what Shelly and I had could be better characterized as an "encounter" than a relationship, because a true relationship has to be more than mutual enjoyment.

Balancing the Boy

At his best, the boy in us genuinely enjoys those to whom he relates. He sees their virtues and appreciates their ability to bring him happiness. The boy in us is a people person.

At his worst, the brat in us uses people as objects for his self-gratification, be it sexual, financial, emotional, social, or whatever. That's why the boyish tendency to take pleasure in others has to be balanced by taking responsibility for others, and this is the contribution the man in us brings to our relationships.

"I JUST WANT WHAT'S BEST FOR YOU"

The man in us takes responsibility for others

Some of the most significant milestones in our lives come when we are handed new responsibility. It's then that our vision can enlarge as we begin to see beyond the priority of our own pleasure or fulfillment.

It's not that we entirely lose our self-interest, but that self-interest is now partially defined by how well we handle broader responsibility. And the broader that responsibility, the more likely it is to start affecting our relationships. We begin to focus less and less on taking pleasure from others, and more and more on taking responsibility for others. As in each of our life arenas, the man in us begins tugging against the boy in us.

Most guys can remember times they were given increased responsibility even better than they can remember anniversaries or birthdays. Remember the first time you drove a car by yourself, or drove someone's daughter on a date by yourself? Remember your first real job? Remember the first big project where you were solely responsible, or the first time you had to supervise someone else's work? Remember the first time you took full responsibility for your own wife, or child? Remember the first time you noticed you needed to start taking responsibility for your parents, instead of the other way around?

I've been told I have a hyperactive memory, but I even remember the first time my mom told me I was old enough to take a bath without her help. The responsibility overwhelmed me. I remember thinking that I hadn't been paying sufficient attention to how everything was done. What if I forgot to wash something? What if I couldn't find a towel? What if my parents moved away while I was alone in there? In a panic, I insisted that Mom thoroughly review each step of responsible bath-taking with me again, and that she promise to tell me before I closed the bathroom door if she and Dad were considering a move.

My relationship with my mom changed irreversibly that night. It wasn't just that she no longer helped me get clean behind my ears. From that moment on, she no longer was welcome in the bathroom when I was functioning privately—a policy we maintain to this day. You see, responsibility can change the very nature of your relationships.

The Disappearing Youth Group

I'm not sure I really felt old enough to be a Youth Director when I was first given that responsibility. I was twenty, and several of the kids in the church youth group were eighteen. Even more of them were twelve—and with that big of an age range it was a demanding job, and would have been even if I had been older.

As I look back, what set me apart from the eighteen-year-olds was primarily the responsibility of leadership. The eighteen-year-olds back at my home church were my peers and my friends. With them I might break curfew, go to a questionable movie, or consider skipping Bible study to go get a pizza. The eighteen-year-olds at my new church were my job, my students, my flock. They were my responsibility. And that made all the difference.

Never did I feel that responsibility more acutely than when we went on road trips. Each time we pulled out of the church parking lot and watched parents waving anxiously in the rearview mirrors, I was reminded how precious a cargo our vans carried.

That's why I was grateful on one summer trip to have my grandparents' house in Kentucky as one of the stops between our northern Illinois church and our destination in Virginia. It was always so challenging to keep track of thirty kids in a hotel, but under my grandparents' familiar roof I knew I could have tighter control. I was also extremely proud to spend that Saturday night in their home, to let them see the youth ministry that had become so important to me, and to show them that another generation was following in the heritage of faith that was so important to them.

129

As proud as I was that night of both my grandparents and my youth group, I couldn't have matched my granddaddy's pride the next morning as the whole group got ready to go to church with him. Though he was approaching eighty, there was a spring in his step and a twinkle in his eye. My grandmother told me later that he was so excited he got up and got dressed for church at 5:00 A.M.

It was a warm summer morning, and I decided to gather the whole gang out on Granddaddy's big wooden front porch to take a group photo. I was already picturing the framed copy I'd send to my grandparents as a thank-you gift. Of course, getting thirty teenagers, youth leaders, and grandparents clustered together and looking at you with simultaneous smiles is no easy task, but eventually I had them all compressed into my camera's viewfinder. As I brought everybody into focus and was about to snap the picture, the entire group disappeared. So much for tighter control.

My immediate response was to check and make sure the lens cap was off. It was, so I shook the camera and twisted the focus dial a couple of quick times before returning the camera to my eye. There was a house and a yard, but still no youth group. Then I heard the screams.

Under the weight of thirty people, my grandparents' big front porch had collapsed. The nails along one main support beam had given way, dropping the floor of the porch about four feet at one end and creating a gaping trap door into which everyone was swept like so many bowling pins.

By the time I reached the group, the kids were already climbing out and helping my grandparents to safety. I was relieved to see that no one was seriously hurt. A couple of scrapes and a lost earring appeared to be the only casualties. We were then able to start laughing about the incredible mishap and go inside to clean up and assess the damage. Granddaddy in particular appeared a little dazed, and we helped him to the dining table, where he sat looking a little disoriented. When we asked him if he was all right, he wasn't very articulate in his response. Then suddenly he slumped over at the table, his face landing on the back of his outstretched arms. My grandmother screamed that he was having a heart attack.

The next minutes were a furious frenzy of activity. My capable youth sponsors leapt into action, calling emergency services and ushering the kids outside. The hospital where I was born was only four blocks away from their house, and though it seemed like hours, the paramedics arrived quickly. I went to the hospital with my grandparents. The other youth leaders took the kids to church, without Granddaddy.

A Changing of the Guard

As I sat in the emergency room of the hospital, I realized how much my relationship with my granddaddy had changed. A few years earlier, he probably sat in this same waiting room thinking about his responsibility toward his new grandchild. Now his grandchild sat thinking about porches, youth groups, heart attacks, and his responsibility toward his granddaddy.

God is merciful, and Granddaddy is still alive today. In fact, it was not a heart attack but a fainting spell from all the excitement that had caused Granddaddy's collapse. Miraculously, God even took care of my guilt. The tests on Granddaddy's heart uncovered an irregularity that could, in fact, have led to a heart attack. Because of its discovery that day, the condition was able to be treated preventatively, with medication.

But my relationship with my granddaddy changed that Sunday morning. I had come into his house the day before counting on him, his home, his church, and his resources to help me with my needs. He had met my needs many, many times before. Now I realized that his responsibility for me was ending, and my responsibility for him was beginning.

I actually visit my grandparents far more often now than I did during youth trip days. I make a point of it. Two or three times a year we plan some vacation time at a nearby lake, where it's easy to run over and check on them. We don't try to stay in their home anymore when we come. Our family of five with three boys under six sometimes makes me slump over at the dining table myself, and I wouldn't want to inflict that possibility on Granddaddy again.

My grandparents are still able to live independently in their own home, and have many local friends and committed family members who help them. So when my family comes to visit there's not a lot that needs to be done, except cleaning out the gutters. The older handyman who mows their yard and rakes their leaves is a little leery of heights and ladders. So whenever we come to visit, I bring my gloves and work clothes. Granddaddy insists on coming out with me and showing me where the ladder is, even though it's always right where I put it the last time. He follows me around the house, and I try not to hit him with handfuls of soggy leaves and sticks as I throw them down from the gutter. He's still trying to be responsible in his relationship to me. And I'm committed to being responsible in my relationship to him.

Taking Responsibility for Others

The man in us derives as much satisfaction in taking responsibility for others as the boy in us does in taking pleasure from others. As we mature, gain experience, and are given positions of greater authority and responsibility, we find that we can make better judgments about what's good for others. In our relationships, then, we seek to bring that good into their lives, even if it means sacrificing what would be enjoyable to the boy in us.

The man in us helps us approach our relationships much as he helps us approach our decisions, our personal discipline, and even our communication. He helps us look beyond the immediate gratification that impetuous actions might bring and more toward the long-term consequences. In the case of relationships, he helps us look beyond our own lives to the effect we have on the lives of others. Weighing those effects, the man in us helps us choose what is responsible, not just what is enjoyable.

In the arena of communication, the man in us helps us speak the truth, even when it's hard. In the same way, the man in us helps us relate responsibly to others, even when that's hard. When our children are sick we make them take their medicine, even though they hate it, and at the time seem to hate us for giving it to them. When a family member makes a bad choice and gets in trouble, we look for how we can help them rather than indulging ourselves in the pleasure of I-told-you-so taunting. When a Christian friend wanders off the path of devotion to God or fidelity to his wife, we lovingly confront, even though it might seem much more enjoyable and safe just to stay out of it. The man in us reminds us to take responsibility for others in good times and bad.

The Authoritative Jerk in Us

My three-year-old son, Noah, likes to make things fly. Usually we can confine those things to the realm of his toys, but there are very few toys, including dump trucks, submarines, and stuffed animals, to which Noah hasn't given the gift of flight. In other words, he makes sputtering and zooming noises and throws his toys through the air.

Teddy, Noah's creatively named teddy bear, was no exception. Beth had just finished giving Noah his bath and was hanging up towels as Noah "flew" Teddy all over the bathroom. Beth urged him to be careful because if he kept "flying" Teddy recklessly he might land in the—and of course as soon as she said the cue, Teddy did in fact land in the—toilet. Fishing things out of the toilet is part of a mother's job description, so Beth dutifully retrieved Teddy, wrung him out, and started to put him in the washing machine. Suddenly Noah was frantic with concern. Teddy couldn't go in the washing machine, insisted our unintentional little hypocrite—he might drown.

Noah had done in his relationship with Teddy what the jerk in us can do when we take too much responsibility for the people in our relationships. We can get so "responsible" for others that we end up trying to control or manipulate them. It's easy to get addicted to controlling people. When you feel you know what's best for someone, it's sometimes hard to distinguish between being responsible and being manipulative. You think they should fly, so you make them fly. You think it's OK to fly in the bathroom, so you influence them to fly in the bathroom. Sometimes even after we've guided the people in our relationships into a toilet of some kind, we refuse to stop controlling. After all, the toilet, however disgusting, seems better than giving up our influence over them to a washing machine.

The authoritative jerk in us is just as bad and excessive as the self-gratifying brat in us. Both seek to make others do what we want for selfish reasons. While the brat may use emotional manip-

133

ulation ("You never play with me!" or "If you really loved me, you'd give it to me!"), the jerk in us uses our authority, power, or influence to make others do what we want.

Balancing the Man

The man in us helps keep us from using people merely for our own pleasure by reminding us that we also have a responsibility to seek their highest good. The man in us knows that we have experience, perspective, and often authority over others that give us good intentions in our relationships. Those good intentions give us courage to influence, to guide, to instruct, and to confront.

But we must not let our being responsible for others drift into seeking to control them. We can't make their decisions, do their work, choose their friends, manage their finances, or live their lives. We must somehow seek their good without smothering them in our own will. And that is only possible when we approach our relationships with humility.

SEEKING GOOD FOR ANOTHER

Without Trying to Smother

HUMILITY in Relationships: Taking Pleasure From Others and Taking Responsibility for Others in the Balance

It's very natural for us to be drawn into relationships because of the attractive qualities we find in others. Most of our relationships start because we stand to benefit from who the other person is or what they can do to please us. The benefits aren't just material or sexual or financial. Our deepest and most sincere relationships are often with those who simply lift our spirits and make us feel positive about life. Some of our richest relationships may be with those who can make us laugh.

The boy in us helps us to look for the many benefits in knowing people better, and to deeply "inhale" those benefits in each relationship. If the boy in us isn't having his proper influence, we can lose the desire to share our lives with others. We can grow cynical and impatient with people, because they've disappointed us so many times before. We can give up on developing new relationships or even withdraw from current relationships, deciding that the effort it takes to relate simply isn't worth the trouble.

Relationships are worth the trouble. That's what the man in us helps us to understand when he urges us to relate even to those who offer little or nothing in return. While the boy in us is looking for how others can benefit us, the man in us is looking for how he can benefit others. If the man in us isn't having his proper influence we may drift from "inhaling" the healthy benefits of a relationship to consuming the person we're seeking to enjoy. If the man in us tries to take too much responsibility, we can end up relating with domineering control, manipulation, or even abuse.

A guy who's striving for maturity in his character seeks good things both from others and for others without the smothering effect of authoritative control. He embraces the attractiveness he finds in other people without seeking to selfishly use them. He freely, even sacrificially offers his care and guardianship without seeking to possess. The mature balance between the boy's desire to take pleasure in others and the man's desire to take responsibility for others comes in approaching our relationships with humility.

A Grilled Cheese Summer

My initial attraction to Marci was definitely physical, but I was surprised at how much I had grown to genuinely like her as a friend. I guess that's why our dating relationship became the longest one of my high school days. Of course, our growing friendship didn't in any way diminish my keen interest in her physical attractiveness.

Marci made the best grilled cheese sandwiches I had ever tasted. Actually, the sandwich itself was an incidental part of what I enjoyed. "Coming over for a grilled cheese" was sort of our romantic code phrase for "come over and make out." You see, our dating relationship spanned one entire summer, and Marci's parents both worked during the day. So as we got to know each other better, Marci would often invite me over for a light lunch followed by a heavy dessert. All we ever did was "make out" (surely there's another teenage word for it by now), but it wasn't long before the words "grilled cheese" alone could make my heart race and my palms sweat.

The Beach and the Hospital

With the fire heating up and the cheese melting scrumptiously in our dating relationship, I began to look forward with great anticipation to my first trip to the beach with Marci. When you're a teenage preacher's son with fairly high morals but at least average testosterone levels, an all-day date with your girlfriend in a bikini is just about as good as it gets. I guess parents know this too, because it took a "double date" with two other couples (is that a triple date?)

to convince our parents to let us go. The beach was almost an hour away, so we set out early. By 9:30 A.M. we were soaking up rays and soaking up each other as we played around in the water.

This particular beach had a huge sliding board built out in the deep water. It was long enough to give you some pretty good momentum and curved up at the end so it threw you several feet out into the water. All over the slide were signs cautioning you to only slide feet first and place your hands behind your head to avoid whiplashing at the bottom of the slide. As I treaded water waiting for Marci to follow me down the slide, I noticed that her hands weren't behind her head. That's why it scared me so much when she came off the slide with a thump, then didn't come up out of the water right away.

Fortunately, there were numerous people who saw Marci go under, so several of us were almost to her when her head finally bobbed up. Then I saw the blood. With some assistance, I was able to get her back to the shore, and soon Marci was walking under her own power.

I had never seen Marci look worse. She had a pained, scowling expression on her pale, makeup-less face, and there was blood flowing out of her scraggly wet hair and down her neck from a pretty nasty cut. We had only been there a half hour, but my weeks of anticipation and fantasies for a day of enjoying Marci at the beach now lay before me like a piece of limp seaweed. Yet I had never been more drawn or committed to a girl than I was at that moment.

Quickly we made arrangements for our friends to find another ride home. Then we bandaged Marci's head as best we could, called her parents and told them to meet us at the hospital, and sped off to have Marci's head stitched up.

That hour ride to the hospital was one of the most precious in our entire relationship. As I took responsibility for Marci's safety, comfort, and well-being, I realized how much more she meant to me than grilled cheese sandwiches and a cute bikini. Her pain was so much more important than my pleasure. Our relationship had grown to be so much more than making out. Everything I had and all that I was were at her disposal now. She was worth it.

Marci's mom and dad met us at the door of the hospital emergency room and ushered Marci in to get her stitches. It was clear she was going to be OK, and her parents told me I could run along, they were sure I had a rough morning. When I told them I'd like to stay at least until they left the hospital with her, they seemed surprised. Her dad in particular raised an eyebrow in a way that made me think I had somehow impressed him.

A little while later we were all able to go in and see Marci. She smiled, and even with her parents right there told me she guessed she couldn't make the grilled cheese she had planned for me later. I told her that was all right, and I meant it. But as I left, I couldn't rid my mind of one lingering thought. Boy, she looked good in a hospital gown.

Relating With Humility and Communicating With Love

If you scan this book's entire list of life arenas and the corresponding list of character traits, you might be surprised that the character trait of love is matched with the arena of communication rather than the arena of relationships. The pairing is deliberate, because the more I've thought about it the more I see love as an action or expression that comes out of an attitude of humility.

God's expression of love to us is that the WORD became flesh and made His dwelling among us (John 1:14). But what kind of attitude governed that expression of love? The second chapter of Philippians says that Jesus was able to communicate God's love in the flesh because He was willing to lay down His own rights as God in order to restore right relationship with fallen man. He humbled himself. Then he tells us to relate to others in the same way—in humility, considering others better than ourselves (Philippians 2:3).

I don't know about you, but that helps me a lot in knowing how to approach my various relationships. It's so easy to be a brat and use others for what I can get out of them, or to be a jerk and coerce others to do things my way. When you tell me to love someone, you're asking me for an expression that may not be possible because I'm still fostering the attitude that I'm better than that person, or that my interests deserve higher consideration. Isn't that what we're doing when we use people for selfish gratification—expressing the attitude that they exist for our pleasure? Isn't that what we're doing when we seek to control and manipulate others—expressing the attitude that we know what's best and that they exist to do our bidding?

But look at what an attitude of humility can do in our relationships. When my desire to enjoy Marci was balanced with an overwhelming sense of responsibility for her well-being, I found my desires and needs bowing to hers. In that hour of crisis, I recognized that she was more important than me, and all that I had to offer should be given up for her sake. No wonder that hour was so meaningful in our relationship. It was faintly mirroring the same attitude that sent Jesus to Bethlehem, and to Calvary.

The great thing about humility and love is that they support and champion each other. An attitude of humility fosters expressions of love. Expressions of love foster an attitude of humility. That means we can choose either starting point in maturing our character and improving our relationships with others. It's in choosing a starting point at all that we sometimes fail.

Jesus and Relationships

That God actually chose to become man is certainly history's most overwhelming demonstration of humility. But even in His daily relationships on earth Jesus added to His cosmic humility many microcosms of the same attitude. Every time His disciples turned around He was relating humbly and communicating lovingly to tax collectors, prostitutes, Samaritans, lepers, thieves—people from whom He had nothing to gain but disease or a bad reputation.

We see in Jesus' approach to people His perfect ability to both take pleasure in them and take responsibility for them. He took pleasure in them not only as their deserving Creator, but as One who could see past their sin to their eternal, redeemed value. Yet bringing those individual souls into right standing with God meant Jesus had to take responsibility for their well-being in a way that only He could do.

Jesus chose both a birth of humility and a death of humility. In between, He demonstrated again and again that mature relationships are those where you value someone so highly and want to enjoy them so fully that you lay down your rights to yourself for their sake. There were many missions He could have undertaken on behalf of our diseased world, and my diseased soul. But He counted our relationship with Him to be of paramount importance. He remained focused on that one most important mission, and thereby showed us perfection in the next character arena—the arena of priorities.

Don't Just Take My Word for It

Taking pleasure in others can be good:

> *I have entered my garden, my sweetheart, my bride. I am gathering my spices and myrrh; I am eating my honey and honeycomb; I am drinking my wine and milk. Eat, lovers, and drink until you are drunk with love!* (Song of Songs 5:1)

———

Using others for self-gratification is bad:

> *For we ourselves were once foolish, disobedient, and wrong. We were slaves to passions and pleasures of all kinds. We spent our lives in malice and envy; others hated us and we hated them. But when the kindness and love of God our Savior was revealed, he saved us.* (Titus 3:3–5a)

———

Taking responsibility for others can be good:

> *The greatest love a person can have for his friends is to give his life for them.* (John 15:13)

———

Controlling and manipulating others is bad:

> *We are not trying to dictate to you what you must believe; we know that you stand firm in the faith. Instead, we are working with you for your own happiness.* (2 Corinthians 1:24)

———

Humility balances enjoyment and responsibility in relationships:

> *Don't do anything from selfish ambition or from a cheap desire to boast, but be humble toward one another, always considering others better than yourselves.* (Philippians 2:3)

Character Trait #6
Focus
in Priorities

...Staying on
TRACK
without breaking
your BACK

THE BATHROOM WITH THREE DOORS

A few years ago, *Psychology Today* magazine created a new subscription mailing that soon became incredibly successful. Primary credit for the package's effectiveness was given to the thirteen intriguing words on the outer envelope, which simply read, "Do you close the bathroom door even when you're the only one home?" This brilliant "teaser copy" invited people inside to the rest of the mailing package, where this and other stimulating questions helped "qualify" them as someone who should subscribe to *Psychology Today*.

I always close the bathroom door. I suppose that means I'm a little inhibited or insecure. I've just always considered the bathroom to be a private place, where modest people take care of their business, and then just like a good camper leave things better than they found them. In fact, our bathroom at home has a novelty guest book in it, where people can register and write notes for us to read later.

For someone like me who values a tranquil, serene bathroom experience, visiting in other people's homes can be a little stressful. This is especially true with people you don't know very well, and even more so when it involves overnight stays and a bath or shower. An alien bathroom forces the most simple, rote routines of your life into a state of complexity. You have to be dressed when you trudge into the bathroom. You have to be dressed when you trudge out of the bathroom. You have to knock before you enter. You have to lock the door before you disrobe. You either have to make sure no one can hear you, cover any unacceptable sounds with running water, or eliminate the sounds all together. These multiple demands can create tension and pressure that make performing normally in an alien bathroom almost impossible.

There's No Place Like Someone Else's Home

One of the many challenging bathrooms in my life is the one at my in-laws' house. Let me hasten to add that the challenges are not in any way their fault, or that of their bathroom. The challenges arise because their bathroom is different from the ones at my house. To begin with, it has three doors. Because it's an older, country home where rooms have been added, one entrance comes from the kitchen, one comes from the hallway, and one comes up from the basement. That's right, the basement.

Two of the three doors don't lock, and of course none of the doors are within reach of the bathtub or the toilet. As a result, it's hard for me to have a completely anxiety-free experience while sitting in there. As I mentioned, I'm sort of a bathroom monk, and my normal activities of reading or meditating just aren't possible in the bathroom with three doors. My eyes are constantly darting from entrance to entrance, my lips poised in case a doorknob twitch or a draft of air threatens my tentatively protected sanctuary and forces me to shout something dignified to my adopted family like, "Hey! I'm in here!" It's like sitting in the Roman Colosseum, waiting to see which door will release the ferocious lion.

You'd think that after a while I'd get used to the bathroom with three doors, and to some degree that's happened. But privacy has grown more and more evasive there as more and more children have entered the family picture. The bathroom happens to complete a large traffic circle that runs from the kitchen to the living room, down the hallway, through the bathroom and back to the kitchen. This gives the kids somewhere to run when they're playing, and of course there's no problem when the bathroom is vacant. But a couple of times when I've dared to "break the circle," I've paid for it. In fact, the bath episode where I first learned the dignified line, "Hey! I'm in here!" was the one where I was forced to grab for a towel so hurriedly that I knocked my underwear and shaving kit into the open toilet.

It's not just the threat of invasion that usually keeps me on the edge of my seat. It's also the messes I tend to make when I'm trying to deal with new surroundings. I'm used to taking showers. But since there's only a tub in the bathroom with three doors, a hand-held shower hose is attached to the spout to help you wash your hair, your neck, or I suppose your hairy back.

The first time I ever took a bath there I turned the water on full force, thinking the tub would fill faster through this little nozzle.

As I turned away from the tub, the overly pressurized connection between the tub spout and the shower hose apparently had more than it could bear. If the shower hose had come completely free from the tub spout, the water would simply have poured straight down into the tub. But it only came partially dislodged, creating a 360 degree geyser that showered the entire room from ceiling to floor, including curtains. By the time I fought my way through the typhoon to the tub, everything in the room was either drenched, dripping, or sitting in a puddle of water. It's the only shower I've ever had in the bathroom with three doors, but it was enough to make me now live in fear of other explosions I may inadvertently create in there.

Managing Multiple Demands: The Pressure of Priorities

Perhaps you're wondering what the bathroom with three doors could possibly have to do with the arena of priorities in a guy's life. To me, it's the perfect illustration of what happens to us every day as we seek to manage the multiple demands of our lives. Just when I think I've got a routine worked out that juggles all my responsibilities and meets everyone's expectations, something happens and the rules change. It's as if the toothpaste is in the wrong place, I can't find a towel, and two unlocked doorknobs are jiggling at the same time. It can be so distracting, I forget whether I'm in the bathroom to shave or shower. It feels like I'm in there just to survive embarrassment.

It's not that I don't enjoy having a lot of irons in the fire at once. I think most of us sort of pride ourselves in our ability to keep a lot of things going and keep a number of people happy. We have our family, our job, our church, our finances, our projects around the house, our hobbies—and somehow every week it all seems to balance. Well, most weeks it does. Well, okay, certain parts of it balance during certain weeks. . . .

The truth is that something is almost always giving way to something else. We so easily overcommit our time, our resources, our energy, our affection, and then looking down the throat of it all we're forced to make some choices. We're forced to prioritize. Some things must be more important and some things must be less important. Some things will get done and some things won't. Some people will be happy with us and some people will be disappointed in us.

When we enter the arena of our priorities and how we govern them, we're getting closer and closer to the core of who we really are. Two guys could attempt to approach their work, play, decisions, discipline, even their communication and relationships in the same basic ways and still they would be very different in character depending on how they prioritized.

Even when we've got the "categories" of our lives in the right order, the urgent things within those categories can push aside the important things. I may decide that spending time with my son is a priority this weekend, then spend most of that time watching a football game with him or doing a project that makes me yell at him more than encourage him. I may decide I have to work this Saturday to get "caught up," then spend the day putzing around with nonessential tasks and fail to dig out at all. It seems you can never go on autopilot with priorities, because the minute you lose focus on the most important thing, a ton of urgent things fills your life like the sputtering tub spout filled the bathroom when I turned my back.

There are a lot of things and a lot of people vying for our attention. How we choose to order our priorities will dramatically influence the quality of our relationships and the effectiveness of our lives. The boy in us is very helpful in this arena, because he can bring a very pure approach to setting priorities. The boy in us gives us a strong determination to do one thing, and to do it now.

"WHEN ARE WE GONNA *BE* THERE?"

The boy in us sets priorities out of a determination to do one thing

The word "priorities" by definition implies that there is a list of things and that there's a need to put that list in order. That's the whole job of prioritization. The wonderful thing about the boy in us is that he has a very short list—usually one item. At any given time, he knows exactly what's most important to him and he's pursuing it with his whole heart.

The women in our lives know better than anyone how we guys can set our minds on something and then pursue it with unwavering determination. For example, our mothers no doubt remember the family vacations where the entire car ride was plagued by the question, "When are we gonna BE there?" Unfortunately, our "being there" was usually delayed by our other single-minded demands such as, "I need to go to the bathroom NOW!"

Our mothers aren't alone. At some point in each dating relationship, we guys can usually convince our girl friends that we have one-track minds. Then they marry us, believing that we'll stay on that one passionate track right on through the golden wedding anniversary. That's when we acquaint them with the other uses of a one-track mind, such as high-intensity TV viewing, or unrelenting quests for a new gadget or toy.

Our wives also know how, on a trip, our single priority is to "make good time," regardless of her desire to see a sight, stop for a bite, or break up a fight (between the kids in the backseat). Our determination to get there in record time also helps explain why we scorn the idea of stopping to ask directions. Every man who's ever driven a car knows that driving faster and faster always makes up for not knowing where you're going. Our wives just need to remember that, from our boyhood, all we've ever wanted from any trip is to BE there.

Hanging On to the End of Your Rope

I've only been sailing a few times in my life. Actually all those times occurred during one week. A few of my co-workers and I were in Washington D.C., attending a convention, and several of our company's clients were also present. One of our guys was an avid sailor, and came up with the idea of renting a forty-foot yacht for the week and taking clients for sails in the Chesapeake Bay.

Once the plans were set, my job was to drive the clients from the convention hall to the boat. I was delighted with that assignment, since it meant I got to spend an extra couple of hours with some very important people. It also meant I went on each and every sail, all week long.

It was while on one of those sails that I received a memorable lesson in priorities. We were well out into the bay, probably a couple of miles, when one of my co-workers started talking about "dragging." None of us had ever heard of this phenomenon, so my friend explained. Dragging was merely grabbing hold of one of the boat's tow ropes and jumping off the back into the water. As the boat smoothly sailed along, the "dragee" (I should have suspected at this point that he was making up some of these terms) could float leisurely behind, enjoying a cool dip in the clear blue waters, then pull himself back onto the boat after he was thoroughly refreshed.

I should probably point out here that my friend worked in sales. And we all agreed that he made dragging sound like invigorating fun on that hot July afternoon. We urged him to show us how it was done. Of course, my friend had just finished eating and wasn't ready to take a dip yet. Perhaps one of us who had just driven out would care to be first? I was quickly volunteered. Maybe my friend did take a dip after all.

As I stood on the back of the boat with the tow rope in my hands, several thoughts crossed my mind. The main thought was how impressive I was being. The anticipatory, almost admiring looks of our clients told me they thought me adventuresome and brave to go first. As I scanned the faces of my deck-shoed audience,

147

I couldn't help picturing the conversation and possible inroads this exciting experience might give me in future relationships with each of them.

There were also a couple of smug thoughts running through my head. My friend had been a little cavalier in his description of dragging, and I had my doubts that he had ever done what I was about to do himself. He had enjoyed the spotlight for a few moments, but I was about to subordinate his flamboyant little splash of words with a dramatic plunge of action.

My final thoughts before jumping were more pragmatic. I wondered how different this could be from water skiing, which I had never done before. I wondered what my chances would be of swimming to shore, given that I had never had to swim two miles in my life. I wondered exactly how deep the water was. I wondered how long it would take a sailboat to turn around, given that you don't just stop the thing and put it in reverse. I wondered if jellyfish would sting a moving target.

Then I jumped. There were four or five seconds of dark, murky silence as I sank fifteen or twenty feet into the bay and waited for the tow rope to pull taut. Then abruptly, violently I was pulled out of the quiet water to the raging waves on the surface. My hands and arms were holding on for dear life, but my face became the main breaker through the salty brine. It was all I could do to pull my head up high enough to keep from swallowing spurt after spurt of water that came crashing into my face.

Instantly, and I mean instantly, every thought that had cluttered my brain on the stern of that boat was totally erased from my mind. In fact, every thought that had ever been in my mind was now totally erased. My singular, determined thought was, *"Pull on the rope. Pull on the rope! Pull on the rope!!"*

I suppose there were technically a couple of side thoughts that crept in there like, *"You're going to drown,"* or *"Don't let go, you'd never make it,"* but I forced them into oblivion with other unnecessary thoughts as I fought for my life against the splashing, incessant waves. When I got within a few feet of the boat, I think my audience could see I wasn't having fun. They then helped pull me into the boat and watched anxiously while I caught my breath.

"You know, the wind is pretty strong out there, and we may be going a little faster than when I've heard about this being done in the past," my friend quasi-apologized. Somehow I wasn't surprised that he had only "heard" about dragging, and that he knew more about sales than sails. But it turned out he was right. When the wind died down later that afternoon, several people tried "dragging" again, and ended up enjoying a leisurely dip in the bay. I expected to be humiliated by the contrast of my panicky experience with theirs, but somehow I wasn't. I was just glad to be back in the boat, and I stayed there the rest of the week. I wasn't going back in the water until I could close my eyes at night without thinking, *Pull on the rope! Pull on the rope!*

Shutting Out the Secondary

A lot of things were important to me that afternoon when I jumped into the Chesapeake. None of them stopped being important once I started to drown. They just became extremely, extremely secondary. If impressing those clients, or showing up my friend, or even contemplating jellyfish had preempted *"Pull on the rope!"* as my top priority, it's quite possible I would have drowned. I don't think anybody knew that but me at the time. Even afterwards no one realized I had almost been buried at sea.

It's the boy in us who can give us that kind of determined, persistent resolve as we pursue the most important thing. Without his help, our vision is scattered. We see the benefits of many things. We believe we can do many things, and lots of them at the same time. Consequently we pursue many things, and we can forget to pull on the rope.

As fathers, we guys sometimes get accused of being "softies" with our kids. And it's probably true that they can "wear us down" a little easier than our seasoned female counterparts. But I wonder if that isn't because we recognize and admire the unrelenting boy in others and want desperately to reward him. After all, that same boy is still at work in us, persistently pursuing the things we've chosen to be really important in our lives.

When our kids come to us again and again and again for a new toy, we see in them the same desire we have for our top financial priority. When they beg us again and again and again to try out for the team, we see in them our desire to compete and excel in our careers. When they ask again and again and again to spend more time with a special girl, we see in them the same desire we have to make our marriage our most important earthly relationship.

When we give in to persistence in others, we're perhaps lending our hopeful endorsement to the idea that wanting something badly enough to forsake other things for it will eventually work! In the midst of lives that can grow so divergent and complicated, the boy in us reminds us that there's always one thing that needs to be most important right now, and he gives us the courage and resolve to pull on that rope.

The Preoccupied Brat in Us

There is a difference, of course, in being determined to do one thing and in being consumed by one thing. That's the difference between the boy in us and the preoccupied brat in us. Like the boy in us, the brat in us at any given time has a very short priority list. His problem is that he refuses to acknowledge that anyone else has a list, or that he may have put the wrong thing on the top of his.

Even as I write these words, my kids are upstairs wanting to decorate our Christmas tree. What should I do? My wife asked me yesterday if I couldn't spend some of my "writing time" writing our Christmas newsletter, which is running late. What should I do? The brat in me doesn't even ask the "What should I do?" question. He just does whatever is consuming him at the time. Other people may have priorities or lists, but they're never as important as his. Okay, okay, I'm going upstairs to decorate the tree now.

Now, where was I? Oh yes. The brat in us is the part of us that can become obsessed. The obsession may be with a goal, a possession, a relationship, even a noble mission. For ninety percent of the guys I know, money is that most likely obsession. We all know guys that have made amazing, stupid priority choices because "things" and the money it takes to buy them crowded their way to the top of their obsession list.

Whether the brat's obsessive preoccupation becomes money, pleasure, power, or even leisure, we can allow his choice to consume us to the exclusion of other important things in our life.

When an important project is due at work, the brat in us tells us to ignore our family. When family life gets too busy, he says it's okay to neglect our church responsibilities. When work, family, and church consume our schedule, he makes decisions that jeopardize our health. The brat in us knows nothing of balance or moderation. His all-or-nothing zeal and his short list of what's important mean he's always abandoning secondary priorities rather than managing them.

The problem is that unmanaged secondary priorities quickly become crises, and crises always threaten even the highest priorities. The marriage that's set aside for the demanding career becomes the divorce that renders the career hollow. The health that's set aside for the rigorous schedule becomes the heart attack that dictates the schedule forevermore. The spiritual life that's set aside for the temporal becomes the hay, wood, and stubble that disappears in the refiner's fire.

Balancing the Boy

At his best, the boy in us helps us sort out what's really important and put it at the top of our list. He brings a persistent, unrelenting determination to pursue the most important thing, rather than be distracted by secondary matters. The boy in us keeps us from breaking our back under the load of our life's multiple demands.

At his worst, the brat in us denies the existence of valid, secondary priorities. He allows us to be consumed with a singular priority that may or may not deserve top place at the time, and almost certainly doesn't deserve top place all the time. That's why the determination to do one thing needs to be balanced with a desire to do many things, and this is the contribution the man in us brings to the arena of our priorities.

"WHO SAYS YOU CAN'T HAVE IT ALL?"

The man in us sets priorities out of a desire to do many things

Just as the boy in us is determined to do the one most important thing right now, the man in us desires to be involved in as many things as he can all at once. Nowhere are these two divergent tendencies better displayed than in front of our TV sets. When captivated with compelling entertainment such as Championship Wrestling or Get Smart reruns, the boy in us can ignore even our spouse's most penetrating attempts at conversation. At other times, the miracle invention of the twentieth century—the remote control—can keep the man in us flipping through four hundred cable channels at a speed faster than the naked eye can record images.

In fairness to the inventor of the remote control, who I understand still receives threatening mail and letter bombs from TV widows, flipping channels is something I was doing long before I owned a remote. My wife will testify to the fact that I used to stand in front of my TV for up to an hour at a time, flipping channels, dodging commercials, and keeping up with three to five story lines or game scores. This always confused and annoyed Beth, who ended up thinking that Matlock had won the final round of Jeopardy by beating Notre Dame in overtime. But each time she challenged me on my ability to follow so many programs at once, I astounded (and continued to annoy) her by recounting with great precision each detail from every show being monitored.

Someday I intend to be able to afford one of those split-screen TVs that lets you watch several programs at the same time. Beth will surely tell me if it gets to be too annoying. I just hope I notice when she's talking.

Smoke-Filled Rooms

When both your marriage and your children are young, it's great to have grandparents who live nearby. Beth and I enjoy the many benefits of having my parents live only about eight miles away, and of course one of those benefits is baby-sitting that is enthusiastic, loving, competent, and of course free.

One winter night, when our oldest son was our only son, my parents came over to our house to baby-sit while we went out to dinner with friends. Our nights out during that first year of parenting had been few and far between, and our then childless friends had been coaxing us for some time to spend a late night out with them like we used to.

New parents are always a little hesitant to leave their only child, but we really needed a break and knew we were leaving Caleb in very good hands. As a special treat for my mother, I kindled a roaring fire in the family room fireplace, and brought in enough dry wood to keep it going all night. For Dad, I parked the TV Guide and remote on one arm of his favorite recliner and two of his preferred magazines on the other. As we set out into the frigid night air, all was snug and secure in our cozy little home.

The dinner with our good friends was delightful. They chose the occasion to tell us they were expecting their firstborn, and we talked for hours about both the joys of parenting and the incredible changes it brings to every aspect of our lives. We speculated about how our kids would grow up together, how they'd be only a year apart in school, and maybe even be close friends like the four of us. More than once, Beth and I fretted that we should get home and relieve my parents, but that always led us into a new conversation about baby-sitting or grandparents, and before we knew it the hour had grown late. We returned home refreshed by friendship and ready to tackle year two of parenting.

The first thing we noticed as we came in the back door and into the family room was that there wasn't much difference in temperature from outside. The second thing we noticed was that my parents were sitting side by side with their arms folded on the couch, wearing their winter coats. The third thing we noticed was the faint smell of smoke. My dad looked exhausted. My mom looked up with a tired smile and asked us if we had a good time.

The good time we had just enjoyed flittered quickly out of our minds. As calmly as possible, I pressed a few basic questions, like why they had their coats on, why it was thirty degrees in our family room, and where our only begotten son happened to be at the moment.

Then the story unfolded. A little while after we left, my dad was adding a couple of logs to the fire. As he reached in and up with one of the logs, he had dislodged the damper from its open position. As it fell closed, it fell sideways, jamming most of the opening up to the chimney. Very quickly the house started to fill with smoke.

The rest of the story, they said, could best be told by taking a tour of our house and yard. Beginning at the fireplace itself, they showed us how the damper was hopelessly stuck, and reminded us that it was a lot hotter to handle and harder to see through the smoke when the crisis first happened. From there they led us to our garage, where they showed us the metal pail Dad had found and used to carry the fire outside, one log at a time. On the front walk leading to our house was what looked like a little campfire. A couple of the logs were still smoldering there.

Back inside, they led us to the hallway, where our dismantled smoke alarm was dangling from the ceiling by two wires. Thinking it was battery operated, my dad had tried to shut it off by pulling and poking at it until finally it came out of the ceiling. When he realized it was electric, he had fanned desperately at it with something—I'm still not sure what—that left black skid marks along the ceiling. Even after they had moved the fire to the front sidewalk, a sufficient number of windows and doors had to be opened before the loud buzzing finally subsided. Why were the windows all still open? Apparently the smoke had really just dissipated shortly before we returned home.

Feeling like we had just toured the set of a Three Stooges movie, we cracked open the door to our baby son's room. He was sound asleep in his bed, still fully dressed, but cozy as could be. The hall thermostat had kept his room nice and toasty warm while it told our furnace to try heating the great outdoors.

Putting Out Fires

After we said goodbye to my heroic parents, closed the windows, and adjusted the thermostat so the furnace would now only heat the inside of our house, we sat in our secondhand-smoke home and evaluated the nightmare-of-an-evening my parents had just endured. Could anything have been done to avoid all that? Would we have handled things any differently ourselves?

Eventually our speculation settled in on one question: "What was the first thing that should have been done?" My snap response had to do with the damper. If they had just known how the damper worked and focused their energy there, a lot of the other complications could have been avoided entirely. Beth disagreed. The fire, she said, was the most immediate and dangerous element of the crisis. They were right to try and remove it from the scene while it was still contained and before the smoke got too bad.

Our Monday morning quarterbacking soon brought us to the same conclusion, however. Many of my folks' frenzied activities had been nonproductive, or at least of secondary importance to solving the problem. Plenty of energy had been expended in efforts that turned out to be of little consequence. Beth and I gratefully agreed, however, that amidst all my dear parents' frantic antics, they had never for a moment lost sight of their top priority. He was sleeping soundly, and safely, in his cozy bedroom.

So Many Priorities, So Little Time

Without the influence of the man in us, our priorities can overwhelm us much as the out-of-control fireplace overwhelmed my parents that winter evening. The man in us recognizes the naivete in assuming that life can be handled one priority at a time. He knows that cozy evenings turn into smoky houses quickly, and that you always have to be ready and able to handle the multiple challenges your busy life constantly deals you.

More than that, the man in us actually thrives on multiple demands. He wants to do a lot of things, to say yes to a lot of people, to be stretched to his full capacity, and make as broad an impact as possible in as many areas of life as he can.

The man in us knows that one-thing-at-a-time guys can be somewhat self-limiting. I had a friend once who would only eat one thing at a time, no matter how many foods were on the table. I don't just mean that he wouldn't mix food on his plate or that he would fill his plate and systematically eat one food at a time. I mean he would put mashed potatoes on his plate, then eat them. Then he'd fill his plate with beans, and eat them. Then on he'd go to meat, and so on. This guy slowed everyone's meal down! We were always passing him something, always cajoling him to take more things on his plate, but eventually we just parked everything within his reach and left him alone. After finishing our meal we'd walk away from the table and leave him, still methodically eating away, one thing at a time.

The man in us has a much bigger vision about priorities than the boy in us. He understands that there are lots of important things in life, and that people often have differing opinions about what they are. The man in us reminds us that we are talented, experienced guys whose capacity for productivity seems to continually increase. We can set higher goals this year because we're smarter. We can be more efficient because we're more experienced. We can say yes to more things because we're better time managers.

The man in us has no greater strength than his ability to organize our many goals and commitments into a master plan that insures their successful completion. With things like a quality staff, a flexible family, a supportive church, and a good calendar, the man in us can show us just how productive and effective our lives can be.

The Distracted Jerk in Us

Have you ever received a phone call from someone and heard them eating something, talking to someone with their hand over the receiver, or clicking at their computer keyboard while they were supposed to be listening to you? Why is that so annoying? Well, aside from the fact that it's rude, it shows that they're distracted. They aren't giving their full attention to the conversation that you feel should be their top priority.

The jerk in us is always distracted like that, always trying to do two or three or ten things at once because he's stretched too thin to meet his commitments. Instead of deciding what's most important and ranking his priorities accordingly, he's trying to do a little bit of everything and being successful at nothing.

I have to admit a lot of my Saturdays can be like that. Throughout the week, I postpone action on numerous things with the thought, "I can do that on Saturday." Then Saturday rolls around, and my own pile of procrastination is added to my family, my friends, the TV, and a dozen new priorities that didn't even exist until Saturday itself did. As I sit back and look at it all, no piece seems bite-sized and no priority seems fun. As I halfheartedly push the pieces around in my mind, some diversion comes along and I end up spending my Saturday doing something that shouldn't even have made this year's list, let alone today's list. The distracted jerk has done it again.

People and relationships are usually the first casualties of an overcommitted life and of unranked or poorly ranked priorities. Tasks and deadlines are unrelenting, but people tend to forgive and grant second chances. So when our priorities get jumbled or unexamined, it's often our families and friends who pay the price. Even more tragically, our relationship with God often suffers even before the humans in our lives feel their neglect.

The jerk in us is always late, always asking for extensions to our deadlines, always making excuses. If there is a part of us that will drive us to bankruptcy, financial or otherwise, it's the distracted jerk in us who overextends himself and needs outside help to do a Chapter 11 reorganization of his life.

Letting our healthy desire to do many things get out of hand is what yields us to the unhealthy jerk in us. Just as the preoccupied brat refuses to see past his immediate top priority, the distracted jerk refuses to admit that top priorities must force secondary priorities or less important things down on the list, or off it entirely. And the guy who can't determine the relative importance of his several responsibilities is destined to fail at all of them.

Balancing the Man

The man in us helps us be optimally effective by managing our life's many important priorities. He knows lots of things deserve our time and energy and he enables us to say yes to as many of them as possible. The man in us is growing, getting stronger and smarter. He wants to be a good steward of our gifts and resources, so he's always taking on more, always striving for impact.

But we can't let our desire to do many things distract us from the most important things. We can't let an overdeveloped work ethic or ego heap more onto our life than it can bear. We have to stay on track with our life's top priorities without breaking our back trying to do everything at once. Keeping the truly important before us while managing the many good things that call for our attention requires an approach to priorities that is perhaps best described as focus.

STAYING ON TRACK

Without Breaking Your Back

FOCUS in Priorities:
Determination to Do One Thing and Desire to Do Many Things in the Balance

We all know that some things are more important than others. In some ways, knowing what those things are was much easier when we were younger. Sheltered by family and school, and largely protected from concerns like finances and health, we could bring great energy to one terrific top priority at a time. A new fishing rod, making the baseball team, winning a special girl's attention—we could camp on each of those goals until it was ours or until we chose to displace it with another.

The boy in us reminds us how rewarding the determination to do one thing can be. Biographies of history's great men seem saturated with this common trait—the willingness to sacrifice everything in order to reach the one thing that was their heart's desire. The boy in us wants us to be great too, and he knows that's only going to be possible if we give our all to the thing we want most.

The man in us, however, has studied statistics. He knows how many golfers there are in the world versus how many make the PGA Tour. He knows how many aspiring actors spend their whole lives as waiters, waiting for a break. So over and over again, the man in us tells us not to quit our day job in pursuit of a single pipe dream. He's also studied those biographies of great men a little more carefully, and knows how many of them gave up their family, or their health, or their conscience, to attain their prize.

The man in us helps us define greatness not so much by the height of the mountains we climb but by the beauty of the mountains we and thousands of others can see from the interstate. For the man in us, the greatness comes when we can point those mountains out to our healthy family, while traveling on vacation in our decent car, which we could afford because of our hard work at our good job, where we enjoy quality friendships with good people. The man in us tells us that a fulfilling life can come in the pursuit of many common things, not just one grand thing.

We need both the boy in us and the man in us to help us set our priorities. We need the boy to tell us that some things really are more important than others. We need the man in us to tell us that many, many things are truly worthwhile. The boy in us helps us set our sights straight ahead, while the man in us gives us much needed peripheral vision. Together, they can give our priorities much needed focus.

Focus, however, is a character trait that must be brought to our priorities both deliberately and daily. Deliberate focus means we know our goals and values. We sit down and concentrate on who we are and what's important to us so that we can consistently point our lives in the right direction. Daily focus means we don't settle for a distant, abstract awareness of those important goals and values. With each sunrise or sunset we take inventory, we reassess, we determine if we're staying on track. Priorities that aren't set deliberately and daily are often not set at all.

You Have to Nertz to Win

My friends and I play a fast-paced card game called Nertz. We've been playing it for years, but my Nertz game has never really improved much.

Like many card games, Nertz requires that you keep your eye on several things at once. Each player has their own deck of cards, which is shuffled by the player next to them and then dealt back to the original player in three groups. The first group of cards is your "Nertz pile." Those are the thirteen cards you're trying to get rid of. The second group consists of four cards dealt face up, where you can play other cards like a solitaire game. We'll call them your "solitaire spread." The third group of cards is the remainder of the deck, which you'll turn over three cards at a time to look for one you can play. (If you're confused after rereading this paragraph once or twice, just skip ahead two paragraphs—it only gets more complicated.)

Besides these three stacks that every individual player has, together you and the other players create "point stacks" in the middle of the table. When the nerve-racking game begins, you can play cards on the point stacks in the middle of the table from either your Nertz pile, your solitaire spread, or your remainder deck where you're turning over every third card. The goal is to get rid of your Nertz stack, but in the process you get a point for every card you play in the middle of the table. (We're almost finished, hang in there.)

You can get rid of your Nertz pile by playing them on the point stacks in the middle of the table. Or you can get rid of your Nertz pile by playing them on your solitaire spread. Playing them in the middle earns you points, but the game doesn't end until someone "Nertzes," or in other words depletes their Nertz pile. Then whatever is left in your Nertz pile counts against you, so it's better to move your Nertz pile to your solitaire spread than not to move it at all. Each time someone "Nertzes," you count up all the points in the middle, on your way to a hundred points (or whatever goal you set). Usually more than one player crosses the hundred point goal during the same hand, and then the most important rule of the game takes over: "No matter how many points you have over a hundred, *you have to Nertz to win.*"

Priorities According to Nertz

Nertz can make me nuts. Especially when you get a group of six or more playing, a high-powered Nertz game can make the trading floor of the New York Stock Exchange look sedate. With all that wild activity going on around you, you're still supposed to handle the deck in your hands, count to three, build stacks in the middle of the table, play solitaire in front of you, deplete your

Nertz pile, and be faster than the other people around the table who are trying to do the same thing.

In such a raucous setting, maintaining your composure can easily fall to the bottom of the priority list. I'm constantly amazed at the words and behavior that a heated Nertz game can bring out of normally civilized people, myself included.

But you know, I'm also constantly amazed at the words and behavior that my heated, complicated life can bring out of me. And I'm most susceptible to such unbecoming conduct when I lose track of my priorities.

I think we guys are particularly drawn to life's "point stacks." Those are the public arenas where everybody's cards are and where we can build up our self-esteem and bolster our ego. Out there in the middle of the table are our possessions, our positions, our power bases. It's really easy to make "point stacks" the focus of our time and energy. As we rifle through our daily deck, our eyes can become fixed on the center of the table where everybody else is playing and comparing and competing. Meanwhile our solitaire spread goes untended, our Nertz pile remains unmoved.

The solitaire spread could represent our more private priorities—our family life, our service to others, our personal character development. When you're building on the solitaire spread, you always find that playing cards on the point stacks in the middle of the table comes easier. That's because when you've added cards to your solitaire spread from your daily "three-cards-at-a-time" deck and your Nertz pile, you have a lot more resources from which to draw. You have more cards to play, more points to score in the middle of the table, and more importantly, you have a place where you can move cards from your Nertz pile until they can play for points in the middle of the table. (Is this the most complicated analogy you've ever had to follow? Please keep trying! The most important part is coming. . . .)

The bottom line is, *"You have to Nertz to win."* The Nertz pile can represent the most central, eternal things on which we build our lives. For the Christian, it's our devoted relationship to God and all that flows from it. You see, cards from the Nertz pile can build and fuel the solitaire spread. They can strengthen our character and our home and our relationships with others. Cards from our Nertz pile can score points in the middle of the table, but the points aren't nearly important as the fact that the Nertz pile is moving.

Cards from the Nertz pile can also remain idle. That's what happens when our focus remains on the middle of the table where we accumulate possessions or position. Or it can happen on the solitaire spread where we build our relationships or even our own character. The Nertz pile can even remain idle just in the routine of counting out three cards from our daily deck of time and energy. Get up, go to work, work, eat, work, go home, eat, watch TV, go to bed—three more cards counted and still no action in the Nertz pile.

First Things First

A guy who's striving for maturity in his character knows that his life must be governed by a clear set of priorities and that they must be in place before he can handle each new day's barrage of decisions. He knows that those priorities must descend from the eternal to the temporal. Eternally worthy God must come first, eternally valuable people must come next, his eternally significant self must come third, and that which decays over time must come last. Within each of those broad categories is room for some individual interpretation, but shuffling around any of the categories themselves can turn our lives upside down.

As we look deeper and deeper inside ourselves, we find the way we approach our priorities very close to the core of who we are. We can work and play with great creativity. We can make responsible decisions and exercise patient personal discipline. We can communicate with love and relate to others with humility. But all it takes is our "stuff" coming before our character or even our family coming before our God to throw our whole character, and our whole life, dreadfully out of whack. The priorities we intentionally or unintentionally choose have that much power over the rest of our existence.

If there is an arena where guys fall down most tragically, it is probably the arena of priorities. It's not that we don't consider the right things to be important, we just don't always put those things in the right order. We can be in the process of trying to be good husbands, then choose to place a TV football game before a quiet conversation with our wife. We can be in the process of trying to be a good father, then choose to work late again rather than come home and play with our kids. We can be in the process of trying to be a good disciple, then give up our time with God to something or someone who can't begin to deserve it like He does.

Jesus and Priorities

People were always coming to Jesus and asking Him what was most important, or who would be most important, or why this or that wasn't more important to Him. Each time He was asked or challenged, Jesus demonstrated that He had His priorities perfectly lined up. In the wilderness, after His baptism, Jesus showed His priorities when He chose God's Word over the expedient alternatives the devil offered. He showed the Pharisees His priorities when He healed a man on the Sabbath and said people are more important than religious rules.

Jesus showed His disciples His priorities when He answered their question about greatness by taking a child in His lap and telling them the first would be last. He showed the crowd His priorities when He told them to treasure the things that wouldn't decay or be stolen, and to serve God as master rather than mammon.

Jesus spent the first hours of each day with His Father, because He knew where His life purpose and direction came from. He spent His quality time with a few fishermen because He knew how the gospel would reach the world. He set His face steadfastly toward Jerusalem and the cross rather than an earthly throne, because He knew what was most important to the very heart of God.

We get the idea that Jesus never vacillated in His priorities because He reviewed them deliberately and daily with His heavenly Father. That daily review must have been the key to keeping His priorities on track for a lifetime. And because of that daily review, Jesus could insure that His priorities were flowing with purity out of the next character arena—the arena of motives.

Don't Just Take My Word for It

Determination to do one thing can be good:

I have asked the LORD for one thing; one thing only do I want: to live in the LORD's house all my life, to marvel there at his goodness, and to ask for his guidance. (Psalm 27:4)

———

Preoccupation with one thing is bad:

Too much honey is bad for you, and so is trying to win too much praise. (Proverbs 25:27)

———

Desire to do many things can be good:

In the same way your light must shine before people, so that they will see the good things you do and praise your Father in heaven. (Matthew 5:16)

———

Distraction with many things is bad:

Martha was upset over all the work she had to do, so she came and said, "Lord, don't you care that my sister has left me to do all the work by myself? Tell her to come and help me!" The Lord answered her, "Martha, Martha! You are worried and troubled over so many things, but just one is needed. Mary has chosen the right thing, and it will not be taken away from her. (Luke 10:40–42)

———

Focus lets you do many things, with first things first:

Instead, be concerned above everything else with the Kingdom of God and with what he requires of you, and he will provide you with all these other things. (Matthew 6:33)

Character Trait #7
Purity
in Motives

...following
DREAMS
without plotting
SCHEMES

SOPHOMORE SATURDAY MORNINGS

My sophomore year in high school was definitely the most enjoyable year of my adolescence. In fact, I know a number of guys who would say the same thing about their sophomore year. I think it's because there's a certain universal relief that comes from no longer being a "scum-of-the-earth" freshman. When you're a teenager you need every bit of self-esteem and confidence you can get, and somehow being a sophomore and knowing you're not the lowest life form roaming the school can make the whole year go better.

That second year of high school was also the one when playing basketball gave me the most pure enjoyment. It's not that being on the sophomore team was all that glamorous. Today most sophomore teams play the preliminary game before the varsity, but my high school was one of the last ones to go that route. When I was a sophomore, we played on Saturday mornings.

A fifteen-year-old guy has to really love basketball to get up at 7 A.M. every Saturday morning of the long winter season. The gyms we played in were usually freezing, the referees were often blowing their very first game ever (in more ways than one), and the only people who came out to watch us were our "faithful-but-yawning" parents. The drive to play any sport under those uninspiring conditions has to come from deep within you. Fortunately, every guy on our team really did love basketball. We ate, slept, and dreamt basketball. During the season, and for much of the off-season, basketball was our life. But the reason that our sophomore year was so special had to do with two key factors besides our love for the game.

Six Cheerleaders and a Good Coach

To be a sophomore cheerleader at our school, you had to love cheering as much as the players loved basketball. In fact, "cheer-

168

ers" would have been a better name for these six girls than cheer-leaders. The word cheerleader implies that you're leading someone else who is participating in the organized cheering process. Our bleary-eyed parents didn't usually bring much participative pep to the games.

As the season progressed, a special relationship developed between the players and the cheerleaders. It was as if we needed their encouragement and they needed our appreciation in order to stay motivated for what were otherwise pretty anonymous activities. After each game, we'd all meet for lunch at the hamburger place a couple of blocks from my house to share and relive the morning's victories or disappointments. None of us could drive and few of us were dating, but all of us shared the dream of making a varsity squad someday. Until then, the camaraderie we enjoyed seemed to make our Saturday morning boot camp more tolerable for all of us. Those six girls were our buddies, and we were their biggest fans too.

The other factor that made that year so special was our coach. Coach H was the only coach I ever had who wasn't a physical education or driver's education teacher. He taught math, of all things, but he was a former college player who loved the game like we did. He soon convinced us that he cared a great deal for us and for developing our potential as well. Rather than forcing each year's team into his favorite offense or defense, Coach H always created new plays from scratch each year to utilize his players' individual talents. He looked at what we each did best, and then crafted those skills into a team approach that was greater than the sum of our individual parts.

Our freshman coach had been a nice guy, but he was also the head football coach. We always got the impression he was thinking football even when he was coaching basketball. Under his slightly militaristic approach, we had finished the freshman season with a record of 5 wins and 11 losses. Our sophomore year the same basic group of guys won 12 and lost 3. That may be part of what made the year special too.

The Changing of the Reasons

A number of things changed after that sophomore year. Some of us made varsity and some of us didn't. We were playing for a new coach. A couple of guys moved away. We were starting to think of college. The style of play got more physical. We could drive, and we were dating more. Things got more physical there too.

But no single change was more significant than the change from playing on cold Saturday mornings to playing on hot Friday nights. Our high school district was one of the largest in the state, and when varsity game time rolled around, we and all our rivals really knew how to put on a show. Home or away, each game was attended by over two thousand people. There was a full pep band playing the latest driving beat, and dance and drill teams helped heighten the hype. Our warm-up suits sported the latest, flashiest style, and we always burst onto the floor through a huge paper hoop that had been hand-painted with our ferocious mascot on it. There was never any shortage of adrenalin during Friday night prime time.

Sometime after my last Saturday morning game, my motives for playing basketball grew far more complex. No longer was I driven just by a love for the game, the support of six cheerleaders, and the approval of a good coach. Now there were crowds and cameras and pep rallies and reporters and press clippings and scouts and scholarship talk. In a way I played for all of them. But at the same time, the more people I played to please, the less sure I grew of why I was playing at all.

My confused motives started showing. When we played on Saturdays, I used to practice hard all week. Now I found myself taking frequent water breaks to talk with the cheerleaders who were practicing in the hall. When we played on Saturdays, I hung on every word the coach said. Now the coach didn't seem to know much that I didn't. When we played on Saturdays, I had post-game lunches with my friends. Now I slept until noon to recover from my post-game, late-night dates.

Instead of the support of six cheerleader friends, I now played for the admiring eyes of one cheerleader at a time. Instead of the coach's approval, I now played to avoid his ire. I hadn't deliberately tried to change the reasons I played basketball. But somewhere along the line, I completely lost the joy that came from playing on those miserable, wonderful Saturday mornings.

Ours Is to Question Why: The Inner Sanctum of Motives

The arena of motives is the first of three hidden, core places where a guy's character is not just displayed, it is molded from the inside out. In the arena of work and play, our character shows itself primarily by how we act independently. In the arena of communication, our character shows itself by how we act in relationship to others. But now as we enter into the arena of motives, we step into those arenas that show themselves primarily in our relationship to God, and are, in fact, quite invisible to others. How we respond to His touch in these hidden character arenas will trickle outward to influence our other arenas. It is before God, in these most private recesses of our life, that He shapes our character into His likeness.

There's no doubt that I was a better basketball player as a junior than I was as a sophomore. There's no doubt I was more popular, more independent, more promising, and more confident. If all you did was look at outward appearances, you'd have to say my junior year was better than my sophomore year. But it wasn't. Why? That's precisely the question that needs to be asked. The "why" we do the things we do—our motives—is an arena of our character that touches and influences all the other arenas, because the "why" factor impacts our relationships, our decisions, our work and play—often with the power to change something good into something bad and vice versa.

Say an old friend calls you and invites you to dinner. That's good. As he serves dessert he tells you he's now selling life insurance and would like to show you a few things. That's bad. Everything is suddenly cast in a new light because of his motive. A guy whips into the gas station and pulls into the pump you've been waiting for. That's bad. When you blare your horn at him and gesture that you were next in line, he grins sheepishly and apologizes for not seeing you. That's good. Once again, motive makes all the difference.

Because you can cover bad actions with good reasons and bad reasons with good actions, motives become a watershed arena in a guy's character. Not only are motives often ulterior, they're often so ulterior that we can't even judge them accurately ourselves. A

171

pastor friend of mine often prefaces personal observations or feelings with the phrase, "If I know my own heart . . ." He'll say things like, "If I know my own heart, I long for a greater spirit of forgiveness," or "If I know my own heart, I could never strike a man in anger." I've always admired his use of that qualifying phrase. He's admitting what I sometimes don't—that I can't speak with a complete knowledge of the forces that drive me to act. My motives can surprise me as much as they can surprise others—sometimes even more.

No, I don't fully know my own heart. But to the degree that I do understand what drives me, I see that there are at least two main camps of motivational forces—inside voices and outside voices. Since at least the fourth grade, an "inside voice" has said to me, "You love basketball! Play it as much as you can." That love for the game motivated me for years to play on gravel courts, with worn rubber basketballs, at rickety, netless rims, with anyone that would play. The inner voice was all I needed. Then that love for the game got complicated by the sound of friendly "outside voices"—six cheerleaders, a good coach, parents—and I realized how powerfully motivated I can be to perform for others.

But the din of both inside voices and outside voices grew louder and more chaotic. At the same time an outside voice said, "Play well to please those cheerleaders," an inside voice said, "Duck out of practice whenever you can so a certain cute cheerleader can please you!" An inside voice would say, "If you take more outside shots, you'll score more points," and an outside (coach's) voice would say, "Pass the ball!"

It's complicated enough to listen to one inside voice and one outside voice at the same time. But each area of our lives has both inside voices telling us what would please us in that area and outside voices telling us what would please others in that area. No wonder we often don't fully understand ourselves why we do the things we do!

If it were up to the boy in us, the voices would be far fewer and simpler, because the boy in us tells us to listen to our gut and follow our instincts. He tells us that Shakespeare was right when he said, "This above all, to thine own self be true." The boy in us reminds us that to be true to ourselves, we must listen to inside voices.

"I DON'T *KNOW* WHY!"

The boy in us has motives that listen to inside voices

In most cases, it's absolutely futile to ask a boy why he's doing something. He usually doesn't have an explanation that's satisfactory, and sometimes he doesn't even have the foggiest idea himself. The more parents expect their young son to have a good reason for his misbehavior, the more flustered they're going to be. And in many cases, the more a wife expects a husband's behavior to have solid, defensible logic behind it, the more confused she's going to be. The curious reality is that lots of times we guys don't really know why we want something so badly or want to do something so much—but you'd better not stand in our way.

Unknown motives can often be the strongest kind, and they are the specialty of the boy in us. The fact that the motive is unknown, of course, doesn't make it nonexistent. It just means it's not fully understood by the one it empowers. It may feel like a drive or an emotion. It may be impulsive or it may incubate inside us for a long time. And in many cases, not understanding why we want to do something ourselves can make our insistence on doing it all the stronger.

It's Like Pounding Your Head Against a Wall

I remember one of my own boyhood days when my brother and I were lying around watching TV. He was spread out on the floor with a pillow under his neck and his head leaning against the wall. About midway through the program, I noticed a pounding. I looked over to see my brother methodically banging his head against the wall.

"Why are you doing that?" I inquired. But he offered me no reply. He was obviously concentrating on his systematic task, and I could see he was mouthing numbers as he pounded. It appeared my brother was counting how many times he could pound his head against the wall. Finding out what possible motive he could have for this behavior intrigued me, so I repeated my "why" question.

"Shut up!" was his terse reply. It came quickly and sternly between pounding out numbers one-seventy-seven and one-seventy-eight, but he didn't break rhythm and he didn't lose count. I was slightly concerned that he was pounding out what little common sense remained in his head, but by this time I was even more annoyed with the hundred and eighty thumps that were distracting me from the television program. If he was going to impose this ridiculous behavior on both of us, he could at least tell me why.

"WHY ARE YOU DOING THAT?" I repeated a third time. Only briefly did the mischievous thought cross my mind that I might be able to break his concentration and make him lose his count.

"Two hundred!" he finished triumphantly. What an achievement. What a marketable skill! He had banged his head against the wall two hundred times, and each thump had been meticulously counted. Now maybe he'd tell me why he did it. No, instead he came over to where I was sitting and started beating the living tar out of me. When my parents eventually came to my rescue and started handing out the punishment, they tried to discern what had provoked my brother's attack. It wouldn't have been unusual for him to be beating me up for a legitimate reason, so my mom was trying to give him the benefit of the doubt while pressing him for his defense.

"Why were you hitting him?" she probed, hoping to find some kind of extenuating circumstances or rational explanation. But I could have told her she was wasting her time. My brother shrugged, took his punishment, and offered no explanation for his attack on me. To this day I'm not sure why he was pounding his head against the wall, or why he pounded his fist into me for asking. I'm pretty sure he didn't even know himself.

What my brother did know was that he wanted to pound his head two hundred times. He also knew he didn't want me to interfere with his agenda, however ridiculous or irrational I might find it. And once I had messed with his agenda, he knew I had to be forcefully educated on what kind of cooperation he expected from then on.

The Often Unsolved Mystery of Motives

Boys have all kinds of drives, hormones, and developing emotions cooking inside. Amidst all the demands and confusion of growing up, it's easy to see how a boy can feel something inside and act on it without ever stopping to consider why he did so. When he's caught up in that "drivenness," he expects others to line up and meet his expectations, to do what he needs them to do in order to meet his goal or satisfy his desire.

These kinds of motives are what make the boy in us passionate in his decisions and motivated in his discipline. He feels a need or dreams a dream and BAM, he's after it with little or no introspection. The boy in us is motivated by those inner voices that tell him what he wants and tell him how others can please him. He doesn't usually hide those motives or exercise great subtlety in communicating them to others. Those around us when the boy in us is in charge know exactly what we want and how they can contribute. Most of the time that kind of clarity can be refreshing and helpful.

A Lap Full of . . . Something

Aside from your basic colds and ear infections, our sons have always been fairly healthy. Our middle guy, Noah, had so little contact with illness his first couple of years that when the flu finally hit him hard he didn't quite know how to handle it.

Beth and I noticed that Noah had felt a little warm when we put him to bed, but he wasn't acting sick and he seemed to go to sleep without any complaints. Then in the middle of the night Noah's cry pierced our sleep. It was more than your average "drink of water" cry, so Beth and I both headed for his room. He was sitting up in bed, with a lap full of vomit.

I'll never forget the first words of explanation that came out of his mouth. Noah looked up at us, then down to his lap, then back up to us. Then he said, almost apologetically, "I sneezed."

Beth and I looked at each other, half struck with the cuteness and naivete of what he had just said, and half struck with the messy job that lay before us. It just then occurred to us that Noah had never vomited before, and that "sneeze" was the best he could do to describe what he was experiencing. While we paused to cherish the moment, Noah's pathetic follow-up question brought us back to reality.

"What do I do now?"

Of course then we whisked into action, comforting our son, cleaning him up, replacing his sheets and covers, and trying to explain to him the difference between sneezing and vomiting. He was obviously a little scared and confused, so we thought a quick physiology lesson would help. But Noah didn't really care WHY he had vomited. He just wanted us to get it out of his lap.

The motives that drive the boy in us can feel something like Noah's "sneeze" felt to him—powerful, controlling, mystifying, and very real. And if someone asks the boy in us why we do something, our explanation might be as profound as Noah's, "I sneezed." Even more likely, our feelings about the things that drive us might parallel Noah's confused, "What do I do now?" Our motives can surprise us as well as those around us. We didn't know we were that brave, or that scared, or that generous, or that selfish. Then an action brings our motive to the surface, and all we can sheepishly say is, "What do I do now?"

The boy in us is often naive or innocent in his motives. He acts on his drives, his instincts, his dreams, with no hidden agenda, no covert mission in mind. He's doing what comes naturally to him. He's doing what he wants to do, and that's often all the reason he needs.

And in many cases his motives are very good. When the boy in us sees someone in trouble, he's likely to leap into action, unsullied with the motive of reward and unhindered by the motive of fear. When he does what's right, he does so instinctively, based on who he is and how he was brought up. When the boy in us is honest, he's honest because he knows you're supposed to be, not because he's weighed the pros and cons of being honest versus being dishonest.

The boy in us is leading out, following his dreams, doing whatever needs to be done along the way, and expecting others to pitch in and help him get where he's going. He shoots straight with people, and isn't afraid to tell them what he thinks. Once they get used to it, people kind of like that. They like being able to see through the words and actions of someone who's not playing games or creating facades. The boy in us may not always have good motives, and he may not even fully understand all his own motives, but at least he's not trying to hide them.

The Self-Serving Brat in Us

Although Noah didn't understand much about his sickness, he learned very quickly how to play it for all it was worth. When he saw how his mom and dad were willing to fawn over him and meet his every need, I think this two-year-old sensed he had stumbled into a gold mine.

Though he was obviously still sick, he quickly developed a self-serving control over his maladies. He needed to lie down, but felt better if it was on a sleeping bag in the family room watching his favorite Disney movies. He couldn't eat anything, but somehow his favorite drink—a "Squirt Bottle"—was all that tasted good. We could take his temperature as long as we didn't block his view of the TV. Each movie was an hour and a half long, and it amazed us how this two-year-old could time and control his vomiting in precise ninety minute intervals. *The Jungle Book*—vomit—*The Little Mermaid*—vomit—*Peter Pan*—vomit—*Cinderella*—vomit. We soon got the impression that all we needed to cure his stomach flu was a movie with a twenty-four hour plot.

When Noah used his legitimate sickness as an excuse to pull his parents' strings, he was illustrating for us the way the brat in us can abuse his boyish motives. The brat in us tends to do bad things for good reasons. He's still unguarded in his motives, still above board in why he's doing something. But he uses that legitimate reason as justification for selfish behavior. He tells himself that because he has a good motive, he can treat people however he wants and do whatever he wants. To the brat in us, the end justifies the means.

177

A Goodwill Gesture

Soon after Noah picked up his stomach flu, our whole family started passing it around. It was on one of those miserable days of quarantine that a couple of neighborhood boys rang our front doorbell. They were raising money for their soccer team, and wanted us to buy tiny caramel candy bars for a couple of dollars each.

Beth answered the door in between temperature-takings, cleanups, and room service, and was starting to look a little green herself. Inside, our boys were crying and the stress was mounting. The caramel bars didn't look good at all, and even though we usually contribute to such causes, Beth told the boys that now just wasn't a good time for her to deal with caramel bars.

The soccer-playing fund-raisers scowled their disbelief at her and turned away. As Beth shut the door and watched them leave through the adjacent window, one of the fund-raisers turned back to the door that he presumed to be without eyes and gave it an emphatic, somewhat universal gesture of disapproval. Little did he know that my wife was still watching, that she had been a third-grade teacher before she decided to stay home cleaning up vomit and answering candy bar doorbells, and that she would have probably seen his gesture even with her back turned. The door flew back open under the suction power of Beth's indignant gasp alone, and she used her best third-grade-teacher voice to tell the boy that she had seen his shameful display and that she wouldn't hesitate to call his mother and his coach and let them know what kind of sales techniques he was utilizing.

You should have seen the brats backpedal. Denying, apologizing, sheepishly grinning, and probably re-gesturing once they got around the corner, they tried to pretend that their good motives hadn't degenerated into such bad behavior. But they had. The brat in them, just like the brat in us, had done whatever he wanted to whomever he wanted, in the name of a good cause. Carelessly, compulsively, the brat in us does the same thing. He acts on whatever motives possess him at the time. And those candy bar motives can sometimes make him anything but sweet.

Balancing the Boy

At his best, the boy in us is forthright and open about what he's doing and why he's doing it. He brings an honesty to his motives that others appreciate and value, whether they agree with him or not. The boy in us is doing what he thinks is right, and expects others to chip in and help him get where he's going. Often they do, because they know he's shooting straight with them about his motives.

At his worst, the brat in us uses good motives as his rationale for doing even bad things. He can be driven by forces he doesn't always understand to do compulsive things that use or abuse other people. That's why listening to our inside voices needs to be balanced with an awareness of other people's agendas. This willingness to listen to outside voices is the strength that the man in us brings to our motives.

"HAVE IT YOUR WAY"

The man in us has motives that listen to outside voices

Just as the boy in us is motivated by what he wants and how others can please him, the man in us is motivated by what others want and how he can please them. Actually, the two motives aren't that different. Both the boy in us and the man in us are following their wants and dreams, but the man in us has learned that everybody has their own wants and that very few dreams come true without the assistance or cooperation of others.

Back scratching is the specialty of the man in us. Somewhere along the line, he learned that the shortest path to his own goals is along the path that helps others reach theirs. If he wants to watch the football game instead of figure skating, he suggests his wife go shopping and buy herself something nice. If he wants something changed at work, he develops a proposal showing how that change will benefit the company. If he wants help in a home improvement project, he makes sure his neighbor owes him at least one favor. The man in us knows which banks he'll eventually need withdrawals from, and he is constantly making deposits into the appropriate accounts.

Installing the Internal "Applause-o-Meter"

Kindergarten is a trap. Any four-year-olds reading this book should . . . oh . . . four-year-olds can't read can they? And the rest of you won't tell them, will you? No wonder it's such an effective trap. Never mind.

What I mean by calling kindergarten a trap is that it's a rather misleading introduction into the educational process. Kindergarten gives you the impression that you're going to just keep doing the stuff you've been doing at home, only under the direction of a different person. Coloring, pasting, listening to stories, playing games and musical instruments, taking a nap—kindergarten leads you to believe you can keep doing what you want all the way through school, then just pick up your high school diploma after snack time.

But even in kindergarten, the subtle indoctrination of the educational system is taking place. You no longer do things whenever you want to do them—you're on a schedule. You're no longer the center of attention—you're part of a group. You're no longer performing for yourself, you're performing for others on a curve. You're now being socialized and systematized so learning can take place efficiently. And during one of those nap times when you're asleep, they install an "applause-o-meter" inside you.

An applause-o-meter is the part of us that responds to things like gold stars, happy-face stickers, and ultimately good grades. Some would argue we're born with one, and there is some evidence in our pre-kindergarten behavior to support that theory. But I maintain that sometime during the early school years, a souped-up version of the applause-o-meter is installed that heightens our craving for praise, recognition, and rewards. I saw it at work every year I was in school.

Elementary Motives

In first grade, a whole lot of what they do is teach you to read. For some reason, I could read when I got there. So not only did they give me these great gold stars and red A's, but I got to read better books than the rest of the kids, and more of them. I even got to skip reading group and do special projects by myself. My applause-o-meter was soaring.

In second grade, things took a turn for the worse. Having never seen anything but an A on my little report card, I was suddenly handed a B− during the first grading period. For art, we were to complete a thematic coloring book each month—in September we colored pictures about autumn, in October it was Columbus, in November the pilgrims. The problem was I could never finish my coloring books on time. I was a fairly perfectionistic second grader, and it was important to me to keep all my crayons in their original slots in the crayon box, with their labels facing forward and their points up. I felt that surely that kind of neatness and precision was more important than any arbitrary coloring book production schedule. But the B− got my attention. My personal artistic preferences must yield to the expectations of the program.

In third grade they lined us up in two groups against the wall and made us spell words until we failed. Then we had to sit down in a cloud of disgrace. Oh, I know "spelling bee" has such a playful, fun sound to it, but you might just as well have called it an "eventual humiliation bee." As much as they taught us to spell, they taught us that the applause-o-meter has a red zone at the bottom where the needle rests when praise and acceptance don't register. We learned to spell mainly because we felt we were only as good as the last word we spelled correctly. Nineteen out of twenty was okay, but only the one who could spell all twenty could stand. And only one third grader sat down to the sound of applause.

In fourth grade, organized basketball started. Fourth, fifth, and sixth graders could try out for the sixth-grade team. That team got to actually wear uniforms and compete against other grade schools. When I was one of three fourth graders who made the team, the applause-o-meter registered strongly with praise from friends, parents, teachers, and the coach. When I became the only fourth grader on the starting five, I thought my applause-o-meter would explode. But it didn't. Oh, the adults in my life were ecstatic and very supportive. But more than a few sixth graders, and even my fourth-grade friends helped me realize that there's only so much praise to juice everybody's applause-o-meter, and that maybe I was hogging too much of it.

Report Card Day

In fifth grade, my applause-o-meter made me a little schizophrenic. I had never experienced the phenomenon of a male teacher before, and for some reason impressing him became very important. At the same time, I discovered that having a sharp wit and a smart mouth brought much welcome laughter from my classmates. So I became a smart-aleck good student.

For example, during a history lesson when Mr. M would ask the class, "What did the settlers at Jamestown get from the mosquitoes that made their colonization of the new world so difficult?"—I'd be the first one with my hand up, knowing the answer to be malaria. Mr. M would recognize my enthusiastic hand, and I would smugly answer, "Mosquito bites." The class would roar, Mr. M's eyes would roll toward heaven, and then just as the laughter died down but before he could scold me I'd give the correct answer. It was a delicate balance, playing both those outside voices at once, but I seemed to be pulling it off.

Until report card day, that is. As I opened my card and started skimming the fruits of my labor, I liked what I saw. A after A accompanied each of the major subject listings at the top of the card, including history where I knew I had most of my best one-liners. Then I got down to the "minor" subjects, like Physical Education and Penmanship. All systems were "A okay" there too, it seemed.

But before my eyes could even fall on the subject listing of Conduct, the big C− stopped me cold, then sent a hot flash of embarrassment from my toes up to my red face. The second-grade B− in art was the lowest grade I had ever received, and I was sure I had corrected all my learning disabilities at that time. My concerns about my grade point average quickly faded into secondary importance, however, when I remembered that my parents had to sign this card. Theirs was one outside voice I wasn't looking forward to hearing.

I briefly considered following the story line from a "Leave It to Beaver" episode and forging my parents' signature on the card. But if the Beaver couldn't get away with it, even with Eddie Haskel's help, I concluded my chances were even thinner. Instead, I faced the music with my parents, and then in one of the most humbling experiences of my life I apologized to Mr. M for my behavior. To myself, I pledged to bring that C− up to a matching A for the rest of the year. But all year long, a B was the best I could muster. Cracking the rest of the class up from time to time was an outside voice I just couldn't completely resist.

Playing for the Crowd

Well, I won't chronicle the development of the applause-o-meter all the way through high school, but it wouldn't be that hard to do. Each of us could recount school days when praise or recognition came our way and taught us how gratifying and motivating it can be to please others and gain their admiration. Probably more than any other time or place in our lives, school gives our "outside voices" volume and credibility. Academics, sports, extracurricular activities, social groups, leadership groups—all these can give lots of people lots of opportunities to excel, be noticed, and feel good about themselves. Once we hear those outside voices, and especially once we hear them cheer, it's often hard for even the strongest inside voices to compete.

I don't mean to make the applause-o-meter sound negative. The fact is that we more effectively learn to read, color, spell, play, entertain, and even apologize because our motive is to please others. The ability to get outside of ourself and understand what others expect is absolutely necessary if we are to function cooperatively and productively in society, and even in our families.

The man in us recognizes that being tuned in to others' expectations is almost always a prerequisite for success. So on the first day of class, whatever the subject, the man in us tells us to learn what it takes to get an A, and then deliver exactly that. On the first date, he tells us to find out what she likes and then bring it to her on a silver platter. On the first day at work, he tells us to find out who and what might help get us promoted. The man in us is extremely pragmatic in his motives, and often when he's in charge we find that we're prospering.

The Man-Pleasing Jerk in Us

From the first Sunday they visited our church, Mark and Jill were impressive. He was smart and charming. She was also bright and very outgoing. Both were attractive and articulate. They seemed to make friends quickly and fit in to our couples' group more smoothly than anyone I could remember.

Before long, Mark and Jill were taking on leadership roles in the group. I guess I was even a little envious of some of the relationships they were building. They seemed to be doing more things socially with our close friends than we were. I wondered why we weren't growing as close to them as others, but I found I couldn't really dislike them, so I just admired their easy social graces and waited our turn to get to know them better.

Unfortunately, that opportunity never came. Almost overnight I noticed that the two or three couples with whom they had been spending the most time no longer seemed as warm to them at church. Relationships that had been cozy only a couple of weeks before seemed strained and awkward. I was concerned, but thought maybe it would blow over.

What blew over were Mark and Jill. One Sunday they gave me a brief, no-eye-contact explanation that they wouldn't be coming to church there anymore because of some disagreements they had with church policies. The next Sunday they were gone for good. Only then did the two or three couples who had grown close to them tell me of the impure motives that had been driving Mark and Jill's friendships. Mark and Jill ran their own business, a business that depended on getting others to buy in with them and work for them. Each of those three friendships had ultimately turned into a two-hour sales presentation, and a life-long disillusionment about charming people like Mark and Jill.

While the brat in us tends to do bad things for good reasons, the jerk in us is the part of us that does seemingly good things for bad reasons. The mischievous brat in us is just doing whatever he feels like doing, and that may lead him into bad things. But the jerk in us is a flatterer and a schemer who is constantly "playing" those around him for his own benefit.

The jerk in us always has an agenda. He's always after something. When he's careless, people can detect his ulterior motives and be on guard. But when he's at his devious best, he's conning even those closest to him. Because he's so calculating, you'd think we'd always realize it when our motives are being governed by the jerk in us. But when he's in control, we often deceive even ourselves and fail to realize or admit why we're really doing what we're doing.

You see, the jerk in us always has an alibi. He has a cover reason for why he's doing what he's doing, and that cover reason is usually acceptable or even admirable. As a result, people "sense" the jerk's insincerity a lot more than they will ever be able to prove it. And that's what can keep the jerk in us pursuing ulterior motives while using the people around us. The conviction rate is too low to be much of a deterrent, at least in this lifetime.

Balancing the Man

The man in us helps us to find and choose motives that are outside our own wants and needs. He helps us tune in to others, and to measure our success by their standards and not just our own. The man in us helps us to be successful in many areas of life, because his motives inspire cooperation and build partnerships in ways we wouldn't otherwise pursue. He helps us to have an objective standard for what's important, what's right, or what's excellent, because others have helped form the standard with their expectations.

But we can't let our motives be so governed by outside voices that we're not true to the legitimate inside voices that oppose them. We can't let peer pressure or group consensus define what's right for us, even if it's more profitable or expedient. Our motives need to move us in the direction of our life's worthy dreams without bowing to devious schemes to achieve them. Sorting out the many inside voices and outside voices that influence us requires that our motives be governed by the character trait of purity.

FOLLOWING DREAMS

Without Plotting Schemes

PURITY in Motives:
Listening to Inside Voices and
Listening to Outside Voices in the Balance

Whatever goals we pursue, whatever decisions we make, whatever way we choose to relate to others, still it's our underlying motives that make our undertakings either noble or sinister. If our character didn't run as deep as the arena of motives, simple behavior modification could probably fix a lot of our shortcomings. We could learn to "behave" in a way that might convince others of our maturity. But it's not that simple. Our behavior is built on our motives, and eventually the "why" always leaks out. When it does, it either anoints or contaminates what we're doing and reveals the depth of who we really are.

The boy in us is tuned in to our inner drives and feelings. He helps us identify what we want deep down inside, and brings to our motives an honest expression of what would please us most. The boy in us can contribute to pure motives because he usually isn't trying to hide anything.

The man in us is tuned in to the expectations of others. He helps us identify what others expect, and brings to our motives a sensitivity to needs outside our own. The man in us can contribute to pure motives because he has learned to submit at least his immediate needs to the good of the many.

We need both the boy and the man in us to keep our motives

pure. The boy in us can tell us when we're playing up to others at the price of our own dignity or integrity. The man in us can tell us when we're so self-absorbed that we're hurting others. Our motives can get soiled easily, and neither the boy in us nor the man in us can identify, much less reach, all the dirty parts by himself. But together they can help us identify why we're doing what we're doing, and challenge us to make the reasons honorable.

Pinch-Hitting for Janna

The first summer I was a youth director, we started the tradition at our church of having a Youth/Adult Softball Challenge. I wished afterwards that I had captioned the event as just a "game" rather than a "challenge," because it quickly took on a competitive life all its own. For weeks ahead of the game, the guys and girls in the youth group taunted their parents and other adults in the church with the specter of their defeat and humiliation.

The adults were good-natured about the softball part of the challenge, but seemed to get a little agitated by some of the kids' barbs about being slow, aged, and decrepit. By the time the date of the game rolled around, the whole church was ready to rumble.

I knew the competition was going to be a little fierce when before the game the two teams disagreed on whether I was an adult or a youth. We compromised by agreeing that I would coach the youth, and could pinch-hit later in the game if needed.

One thing the slightly over-confident youth group hadn't counted on was the male/female ratio. While the youth group had more girls than guys in it, the number of ladies willing to play on the adult team was limited. To allow everyone in the youth group to play, the youth team had to have at least fifty percent girls on the field. The adults had only two ladies, neither of whom lasted the whole game.

Still the game itself was quite competitive. Most of the girls didn't get on base, but the younger legs and arms of the guys gave the youth team somewhat of an advantage. Going into the bottom of the last inning, the youth team was trailing by only one run. With runners on second and third and two outs, I looked up to see whose shoulders our hopes would rest on. It was Janna, a skinny little seventh-grade girl.

The inside and outside voices started competing for my attention. Inside: I told myself I wanted to win. Seize the opportunity, pinch-hit for little Janna and win the game. Outside: one of the youth sponsors read my mind and said, "You're going to let Janna bat aren't you?" Inside: I reminded myself of the reasons I was doing youth ministry and how this decision might impact this impressionable young girl. Outside: a chorus of teenage voices urged me to step to the plate and back up their boasting.

It suddenly occurred to me that Janna might be scared to death to step up to that plate. What kind of seventh-grade girl would invite that kind of pressure? I walked over to her and asked her if she'd like me to bat instead of her. She told me if I tried she'd kick me in the shin. Her spirited retort was answered by an onslaught of boos from the youth group. Out on the field, the adults were jeering us to let the little girl bat. With one more quick check of my motives, I decided to let Janna bat.

I wish I could tell you that Janna stepped up to the plate and knocked in the winning run. But she grounded out to third base. Oh, it was a screaming grounder that brought everyone to their feet and almost went through the infield. The guy on third had to make a nice play on it. But it was still an out, and the youth still had some crow to eat for their weeks of trash talking.

I'm not sure if anyone else would remember that game or not. I don't even think Janna would—she went on to be a star collegiate volleyball player who would still kick me in the shin if I tried to play in her place. That's the funny thing about acting on pure motives. Lots of times the results seem inconsequential and go unnoticed by everyone except the one who has to sort through the voices.

Wearing Your Favorite Underwear

Before I sat down to write these pages on motives, I did something I'd like you to know about. I changed my underwear. Why did I change my underwear? Well, mostly to make you smile I suppose. But also to make a point.

You see, I have some favorite underwear. Let's be honest now, most of us do. My favorite underwear is the newest stuff in the drawer. I hate it when I get hold of an older T-shirt that has shrunk up over time and pulls at my armpits. Even worse are shorts that have lost their elastic in places and that pull, creep, or fall in all the wrong places. When I break open a new package of underwear, my whole day seems to go better.

The problem is that laundry at our house is done on a fairly regular basis, and my underwear is stacked in a dresser drawer. That means that unless I'm careful, I'll wear the same underwear over and over and over again. Why don't I just take underwear from the bottom of the stack? That presents a whole different problem. At the bottom of the stack is the emergency underwear. That's the stuff you should have thrown away years ago. It's frayed at the edges, one or two sizes smaller than you are now, and no longer close to its original color. Emergency underwear is best for polishing your shoes or waxing your car. If you're forced to actually wear it, you'll be miserable and probably walk funny all day long.

A "Brief" Look at Pure Motives

I think our underwear is a pretty good symbol for our motives. Like underwear, our motives are something we have to examine carefully at the outset, because once they're selected we're kind of committed to them. No matter how uncomfortable they may feel midway through the day, they're ours for the duration. In a drawer full of inside voices and outside voices, it's easy to get hold of the wrong motive, and in doing so we can adversely color any undertaking, however noble it may look to others.

Like underwear, our motives are hidden to all but those closest to us. Yet they have such power over our entire being! On the days I accidentally put on a pair of emergency underwear, my whole attitude and demeanor can change. Because I'm not comfortable on the inside, what's happening on the outside can be tainted as well. But what can I do? Tell the people around me I'm having a bad underwear day? No, I keep them hidden, embarrassed of what's inside but still committed to the underwear, or the motive,

I've chosen. I tell myself I'll choose a better motive tomorrow, that I won't keep living a contradiction. But when I get home, I don't throw the old stuff away—I might need it again some day.

When we're shuffling through the motive drawer of our character dresser, we need to sort past all the impure, self-serving inside voices. We need to avoid all the equally impure, man-pleasing outside voices. If we've kept up-to-date on our laundry, there are some pure motives in that drawer, motives that serve others and honor God. Like fresh, new cotton, they're unsullied with selfish pleasure. Like snug, flexible elastic they're adaptable to the needs and expectations of others.

The challenge, of course, comes in taking the time and effort to discern what we're taking from the drawer. That's why I went to change my underwear before writing this. I'm wearing the best pair I own. And you know what? I'm going right now to throw out the unnecessary emergency stuff that only makes me uncomfortable and gets me in trouble.

100 Percent Pure?

When we sold our house recently, we had to have our well water tested for impurities. The test came back with a reading of two parts bacteria per thousand. The inspector assured us that was hardly worth worrying about, and that a bag of chlorine down the well should take care of that small trace of impurity.

We did as he suggested and then paid to have another test run. There were still two parts bacteria. We were puzzled and asked the inspector how such a small trace of bacteria could survive the chlorination. "You know, I've quit trying to figure these darn things out," was his expert reply. But he agreed to come out and retest the water again for free, in case he or the lab had made some mistake. Apparently they had. The next reading came out pure.

Is it possible to have motives that are completely pure? And even when they seem pure to us, is it possible that our ability to know our hearts and test our motives is less than perfect? I'm not sure I know the answer to those questions. But I do know that the buyers of our house weren't satisfied until we had done our level best to test the water and remove every impurity we could find.

Our motives may never be free from every known impurity in this lifetime, but a guy who wants to develop maturity in his character will make sure his motives are tested and treated to the very best of his ability.

Jesus and Motives

Jesus took the subject of motives very, very seriously. I think He got that from His Father. Nowhere in the Old Testament do you see God more fiery-eyed than when His puny people challenge His motives. Whether it's the Israelite people asking WHY they were led out of Egypt, the psalmist asking WHY the wicked prosper, or Job asking WHY he was allowed to suffer, God always responds to the "why" question with a "who" answer. His character is righteous and holy, and therefore His motives are unquestionably pure.

In the same way, Jesus' most heated words were directed against the hypocritical religious leaders who claimed righteousness but reeked of rotten motives. Jesus called them snakes, tombstones, and dirty cups, all as a way of pointing to their hypocrisy. He said that the deeds and righteous acts of which they were so proud were empty and hollow. But none of Jesus' indictments against these religious leaders was more penetrating than the one recorded in Mark 7:13, where Jesus says, "In this way the teaching you pass on to others cancels out the word of God. And there are many other things like this that you do."

Jesus' own motives, however, were always transparent and pure. When His parents lost track of Jesus in Jerusalem at age twelve, then found Him lingering in the temple, they asked Him WHY He had worried them so. Jesus' reply was that their search could have begun in the temple, because they should know that His motive was to be about His Father's business. Mary and Martha wondered WHY Jesus allowed their brother Lazarus to die, then marveled as Jesus' motive of glorifying God worked a miracle over death. Sarcastic passersby taunted Jesus on the cross and asked Him WHY He didn't save himself. If they had been paying attention to His consistent, pure, lifelong motives, they would have been praising God that He stayed on the cross and died.

On the cross, Jesus showed that the reason you do something ultimately flows from what you've determined to be supremely important. His motives were an arena of His character that flowed freely from an even deeper character arena—the arena of values.

Don't Just Take My Word for It

Following your own inner motives can be good:

> *If anyone makes himself clean from all those evil things, he will be used for special purposes, because he is dedicated and useful to his Master, ready to be used for every good deed. Avoid the passions of youth, and strive for righteousness, faith, love, and peace, together with those who with a pure heart call out for the Lord to help.* (2 Timothy 2:21–22)

———

Self-serving motives are bad:

> *You may think that everything you do is right, but remember that the* LORD *judges your motives.* (Proverbs 21:2)

———

Meeting others' expectations as your motive can be good:

> *Among the weak in faith I become weak like one of them, in order to win them. So I become all things to all men, that I may save some of them by whatever means are possible.* (1 Corinthians 9:22)

———

Man-pleasing motives are bad:

> *Make certain you do not perform your religious duties in public so that people will see what you do. If you do these things publicly, you will not have any reward from your Father in heaven.* (Matthew 6:1)

———

Balancing inner desires with outside expectations can help produce pure motives:

> *Our appeal to you is not based on error or impure motives, nor do we try to trick anyone. Instead, we always speak as God wants us to, because he has judged us worthy to be entrusted with the Good News. We do not try to please men, but to please God, who tests our motives.* (1 Thessalonians 2:3–4)

Character Trait #8
Discernment
in Values

...embracing
TODAY
in an eternal
WAY

THE DREAM CAR

I don't think I've ever talked to a guy who didn't have a dream car. I know some girls probably have them too, but with guys it seems to be a universal, perhaps genetic phenomenon. We tear out pictures of our dream cars. We read magazine articles about them. When we see our dream car on the street, we create hazardous traffic conditions just to be able to pull up alongside it. Gazing at our dream car, even when someone else is driving it, is like taking a long, cool drink on a hot day. It won't completely satisfy you and you'll want more later, but for the moment, boy is it good.

Naturally, the standard for our dream cars tends to get higher as we get older. I've had three dream cars in my life so far, and each one has been monumentally more expensive than its predecessor. That's part of what makes it a dream car. It's always just out of reach financially. If you can afford it, you buy it and choose a new one. A dream car has to be elusive.

My Kingdom for Some Horsepower

Of course when we're sixteen, almost every car in the world is elusive. That's why at that age we usually choose two dream cars—one that's hopelessly unaffordable and one that's affordable by our parents if they'd help us buy it. In most cases, the two cars are still equally elusive.

That certainly was the case at our house when I was sixteen. Even a few hundred dollars for a used car was out of the question. And with a brother two years older than me, my chances of having my own car any time soon was practically nil. Our family did have two cars, but between my parents and a brother with a part-time job and a full-time girl friend, I didn't get much time behind the wheel. Getting either a job or a steady girl friend didn't seem worth the trade-offs to me, but still it was discouraging to know how to drive and get so few opportunities.

Then my hopes were lifted. An older man at church named Joe, who had always taken a special interest in me, started asking me about getting my license and whether I ever got to use the car much. I sang him my sad song, and he lamented along with me about being one of several children and being low on the automotive pecking order. Joe told me he might be able to help me someday, but didn't give me any specifics. I appreciated his empathy, but figured I'd find a way to a car on my own long before his help would ever pan out.

Then one summer day three months after I got my driver's license, Joe pulled into the driveway while I was outside shooting baskets. He hopped out of the car and handed me the keys. My adrenalin rushed. He went on to explain that this old car of his needed a little work, but that if I was willing to put some time into it, he'd sell it to me for twenty-five dollars.

Twenty-five dollars! Twenty-five dollars!! I had that much money. I wouldn't need my parents' financial backing. *Ergo, ipso facto* (my mind raced in Latin), I might not even need their permission! How could they say no to a deal like this? I jumped into the car with my fairy godfather and off we went for a spin.

You Get What You Pay For

I was barely sixteen, and the vehicle I had just adopted as my dream car was twelve. It was an old Ford Falcon, with a manual three-speed transmission on the steering column and no power features, especially under the hood. Joe had to show me how to drive it. In fact, he had to show me how to nurse it into starting. Once we got underway, it sounded more like a helicopter than an automobile. But my affection for that car was immediate and passionate.

When we returned to the house, Joe's wife was waiting for him in their other car. He told me he'd leave the Falcon with me while I talked it over with my parents. If I decided I wanted it I could pay him next Sunday.

The next three days were a tug-of-war in epic proportions at my house. I championed the cheap price, the convenience of having a third car, the peace it would bring between my brother and me, and the opportunity to learn automotive maintenance. My parents championed the cost of insurance, the cost of gas, the cost of repairs, and the cost to my schoolwork and sports plans in the fall.

On the first of those three days, my buddies and I drove around the neighborhood in that old car, basking in our independence and dreaming of the exploits we'd have in this dream machine. Our high school mascot was a falcon, and we talked about how cool it was to have that kind of car. Then on day two, the muffler that was half attached became fully detached. As we drove around, neighborhood kids would yell unkind things like, "Get a horse!" By the third day, my friends had stopped calling the car "the Falcon" and started calling it "Uriah" because it was such a heap. By the time Joe came to repossess my dream car, he had to jump start it to take it home.

Discerning What's Important: Our View Through Our Values

It hurt my heart to watch Joe drive away in my Falcon-turned-Uriah dream car. When you're sixteen, very few things in the world are more important than the freedom and independence that come with driving. Your world seems more and more crowded and demanding, and the authorities in your life seem more and more restrictive. To be able to escape—to just go somewhere in your own set of wheels, listening to your own music with your own friends—can seem really important.

When you're the parent of a sixteen-year-old, however, different things are important. Your world seems more and more out of your control. Your kids want more and more things and more and more independence. Your basic needs cost more and more money. At the same time, it seems you have less and less time to meet your own goals and responsibilities. You're less and less sure that things are going to work out exactly the way you plan them. To be able to spare your son some frustration—to steer him clear of an expensive mistake, to have one less thing in your life and your driveway to worry about—can seem really important.

At the time I couldn't understand why my parents wouldn't let me spend my twenty-five dollars. They probably couldn't understand why I'd want a twelve-year-old, money-sucking heap named Uriah. And as we locked horns and sought to get underneath each other's motives, we entered one of the deepest character arenas—the arena of values.

If the arena of motives is represented by the simple question, "Why do we do the things we do?" then the arena of values seems equally simple. The values question is simply, "What's really important?" However elementary these questions seem, we all know them to be among the deepest in life. And how we choose to answer them has far-reaching implications in the development of our character.

Some of our values are little more than skin deep. We like blue better than red, pizza better than asparagus, the Cubs better than the Mets. These aren't the values I'm talking about. There are substantial, life-regulating values that run very close to the core of our character along with our motives. In fact, our life values are even closer than our motives to the core of who we are, because whether we realize it or not, our motives flow continually out of our values.

When we do things that are motivated by money, it's because we've determined that money is important. When we do things that hurt our career for the sake of our family, it's because we've determined that our family is more important. If we choose to be in conflict with our family for the sake of being true to God's Word, it's because we've chosen to value one very important thing even higher than another.

Our character in the values arena trickles down and affects all the other arenas in addition to motives. Discerning what's truly important helps determine what our priorities will be. Our values influence how we will approach our relationships and how much effort we'll make to communicate lovingly. Those same values will show us where to direct our personal discipline. And when we're careful and thoughtful enough to consult our values first, our decisions become much easier and more consistent.

Well-established values can help us navigate life with confidence and direction. The problem is that we often leave our values as neglectfully unexamined as our motives. That doesn't mean we stop having values. It just means we can let them drift along with the influences around us.

The Dream Car's Memorial Trunk

I mentioned earlier that I've had three dream cars in my life so far. I've been driving one of them for over seven years now. I wanted my little red car for three years before I felt I could afford it. It's the only new car I've ever owned. Now, with 85,000 miles on it, I'm just starting to dream again.

If you were to look at my little red car, you might wonder what's so dreamy about it. Aside from its obvious age and wear, the paint on the car is rather two-toned. I had to have the trunk and rear quarter panel replaced and repainted about a year and half after I got the car. They were wiped out in a collision that almost cost me my life.

I'll spare you the details of the accident, though I could replay each detailed second to this day from the slowed-down recording my mind made of it. Suffice it to say it was at fifty miles per hour on a rainy day, and I crossed six lanes of traffic in the process.

If you've ever been in a life-threatening accident, you know how it can get your attention and make you think about your life and what's really important. I remember that even though I had been on my way to work when the accident occurred, I drove my banged-up dream car directly from the accident scene to the school where my wife taught. School hadn't started yet, and I was able to go to her classroom and take her outside to see my banged up, eighteen-month-old dream car.

I knew it would be important for her to see that I was all right, and that's part of why I went in person to her school instead of calling her with the news. Even having seen I was okay, Beth still shed tears for my loss. She knew how important that car was to me. But that morning the car had practically lost all importance as the accident forced me to look deep inside for my real values. That inside look had convinced me to drive to Beth's school right then. I was admittedly a little scared over what had almost happened, and I needed to get out of the dream car and be in the presence of the person who was really most important to me. Decisions like that about core values are best made by the boy in us, because it's the boy in us who reminds us that tomorrow is not guaranteed, and that our values should reflect the importance of the immediate.

"GIMME THAT!"

The boy in us values the immediate

Boys love treasure. That love can sometimes be quite distracting for us grown-up boys, and lead us into all kinds of vices. But listen to a young boy define treasure and it will make you long for the days before you understood interest rates, bond markets, and the Dow Jones Industrials.

I remember my boyhood treasure box (it was actually an old metal tackle box) was filled with my favorite rocks, my baseball cards, a bunch of rubber bands, and a keyring full of keys that didn't unlock anything. My wife thought me a little daffy when I suggested buying a couple of plastic tool boxes for our five-year-old and three-year-old boys. But since we've brought our third little boy into the world I've been surprising her with all kinds of silly boyish wisdom. Our guys now love their treasure boxes. They've been filling them with things from the Everything's A Dollar store.

There are several great things about the dollar store. Of course the price is right. The selection is impressive too—it's amazing the number of things you can price under a dollar and still make a profit. But the greatest thing about the dollar store is that it makes Dad look rich. I can walk in there with my sons and fearlessly say, "Pick anything you like. Nothing's too good for my boys."

Keep in mind that our guys are too young to understand much about money. To them, a one dollar bill is the same as a one hundred dollar bill. The contents of the dollar store is as spectacular as that of an expensive department store. My boys are still at the stage where they look at a stack of pennies on my dresser and say, "Wow, Dad, you're rich!" And when they do, I allow myself to enjoy it and maybe even believe it, just for a moment. And why not?

As far as their immediate concerns are, I am rich. And I love showering my wealth upon them, especially at the dollar store.

Unfortunately, our guys are growing up very quickly. And even though they don't understand our monetary system, the dollar store is still teaching them a few things. The last time we went there, I handed each of the boys their dollar and told them to go crazy. When they brought their selections to the counter, I asked them where the dollars I had given them were. My industrious three-year-old looked up at me and said, "They're in my pocket. We want to use YOUR dollar."

Here Today, Gone Tomorrow

To the boy in us, treasure is immediate, accessible, and to be enjoyed right now. When you tell him that anything worthwhile is worth waiting for, he replies that nothing worth waiting for could really be that important. His values are focused on the here and now, and as a result his life is enviably free of anxiety and stress.

Five-year plans, thirty-year mortgages, long-term investment strategies—these are all boring to the boy in us. He'd rather go to a movie, spend time with friends, or just have a good day at work. Time is precious, life is short, and trying to live in the future is futile. The boy in us reminds us that a high percentage of our worries never come to pass, and we have only high stress and high blood pressure to show for them.

The boy in us can make us feel rich in the same way my sons make me feel rich at the dollar store. He reminds us that we have all we need for today, and that the world is a store where a dollar's worth of optimism can buy almost anything. There's something liberating, even eternal about living only in the present, and the boy in us helps us rediscover the tremendous joy of living one day at a time.

Walking Around the Block Slowly

My family lives in a fairly secluded area, with very little thru traffic. It's a great neighborhood for walking. Before we had children, Beth and I walked all the time.

After the baby invasion, Beth and I still walked the neighborhood for exercise or for alone time, but those became solo walks early in the morning or late at night. As the boys got older and learned to walk themselves, Beth started taking them for daytime excursions into the neighborhood. One Saturday she suggested I do the same. She had endured a particularly tough week, it seemed, and needed some space and time alone. I knew that was the case when she delivered her usual code phrase: "These boys need their daddy today." Pretty subtle code phrase, isn't it?

The boys and I were hardly out of the driveway, however, before I was getting frustrated. They had wanted to bring along their favorite stuffed animals, their toy swords, their favorite jackets, and several rocks to throw in a nearby pond. Before we made it to the first corner I was carrying everything and they were roaming everywhere.

Part of the problem was that every one of my steps required three to five of theirs. Even if they had been halfway purposeful in their walking, the pace would have been painstakingly slow. I had already told them where we were going, and I was anxious to get there and have some fun. They couldn't have cared less where we were going. For them, fun was something that happened along the way. Sticks, rocks, leaves, flowers, doggie doo, birds, birdie doo— anything they could find to pick up or poke at was a worthwhile distraction.

I was trying to be patient as I coached them along our walk. I told them where we were going. I told them what lay ahead at the pond. I told them we needed to hurry because Mommy would miss us. I told them that if they didn't get their little behinds in gear . . . well, you get the point.

They, however, didn't get the point. I think they were trying to understand my futuristic task-orientation, but nothing I could promise them could compete with the joys they were discovering moment by moment along the way. An hour and a half later, we had circumvented the block where we live one time. I gave up on the pond entirely, and discarded the unused rocks on my way into the house. I don't think they even noticed.

Blockbuster Values

As I ushered my two little slowpokes back in the door after our walk, I started dumping my frustration on Beth. I asked her how she ever got anything done at the pace these guys moved. I asked her if they ever cared enough about the pond to actually get there. I suggested that next time we went I'd take their little red wagon and pull them instead of letting them walk. At least we'd reach our destination that way.

As you might guess, Beth didn't look particularly surprised at my experience, nor did she act particularly empathetic. In the same patient, teaching voice I'd heard her use so many times on her other two boys, she asked me why I had taken them on a walk in the first place. Well, of course it had been to give her a break and to spend some daddy time with them.

"Then your objective wasn't to get to the pond?" she continued. I began to feel like the black king just before he's checkmated by the white queen. No, the pond had just been something I thought they'd enjoy doing. Beth graciously acknowledged that they probably would have enjoyed it, and that it was a good idea. But she had been given an hour and a half to herself and the boys had been given an hour and a half with their wonderful though slightly impatient daddy. Hadn't our objectives been met, even short of the pond?

Caleb and Noah, who had been naively watching this interchange like a Ping-Pong match, looked innocently to me to see how I'd return this volley. Instead I knelt down to their eye level and told them I was sorry for being impatient with them. Then I asked them if they'd like to go try and find that pond again. They squealed their delight, and we headed back out the door as I smiled my appreciation to my more experienced toddler-walking wife. For her wisdom she received another hour and a half alone, and I don't remember if we made it to the pond the second time or not.

The Nearsighted Brat in Us

I have a few memories from my own boyhood about going around the block. It was before I had my first bike, but my older brother's friend had one, and he would occasionally give me a ride around the block on the back of his bike. I thought that was great fun, and my brother's friend knew it. That's when he introduced me to his convenient payment plan.

During my few short years, I had accumulated a decent collection of comic books. I shudder now to think what they would be worth if I had kept them, and they were pretty valuable to me even then. But those rides around the block on a bike I didn't have were pretty alluring, too. One comic book at a time, I traded my collection to my brother's friend (notice I'm not calling him *my* friend?) for rides around the block. In a matter of days, my comic book stack was gone, my brother's friend was gone, and all I had left were faint memories of a few spins around the block.

While my brother's friend could be accurately labeled as a brat, it was my behavior that illustrates the way the brat in us approaches the arena of values. While the boy in us can give us a healthy focus on the importance of the immediate, the brat in us can convince us to live only for the moment. His values are deliberately temporal and irresponsibly nearsighted. What's important to him is what he can consume or enjoy today, regardless of long-term consequences or trade-offs.

The brat in us would identify with Esau, who thought nothing of giving up his birthright to Jacob for a good bowl of stew. Birthrights are tomorrow things and stew is a today thing. The brat in us tells us to only worry about today.

The brat in us thinks about eating, but not about getting fat. He thinks about production, but not ecology. He thinks about sex, but not pregnancy. He thinks about sin for a season, but not separation from God.

When the brat in us is controlling our lives, we're either having a temporary great time or miserable hangover. His values are those that lead us to terrible decisions, upside-down priorities, and impure motives. His nearsighted values have far-reaching effects on the whole of our character, and the whole of our life.

Balancing the Boy

At his best, the boy in us is free from cumbersome worry and anxiety about the future. He recognizes that most of life is just walking around the block, and he reminds us that the truly important things are what you do along the way. So he stops and smells the roses. He tells us it's okay to relax, to enjoy our family and friends, to take a nap, to let go of a burden. He values what is immediate because his Father is rich and the dollar store is full.

At his worst, the brat in us treats the future as if it didn't exist. He spends all he has and seizes all he can reach. His minimum daily requirements are inexhaustible, because every day is given to gusto. That's why the value we place on the immediate has to be balanced with the value we place on the eventual. And that longer view of what's really important is the contribution of the man in us.

"ONE OF THESE DAYS . . ."

The man in us values the eventual

In the same way the boy in us is focused on the present, the man in us is focused on the future. The man in us values that which is good for the long haul. He buys brand names and extended warranties. He changes the oil in his car every two thousand miles. He cleans his tools before he puts them away. His favorite suit is classic navy blue. He flosses his teeth regularly.

To the eventual-minded man in us, an ounce of prevention is worth a pound of cure. So he protects his car by parking it in the most remote corners of shopping mall parking lots. He takes his vitamins religiously. He makes motel reservations six months in advance. He knows exactly where all his money is invested, and keeps a meticulous ledger of all the interest he's earning. But you never, ever speak to him of touching the principal.

Four Degrees, Fair in Height

The year my little sister graduated from college, four generations from our immediate family convened in that western Kentucky university town in a reunion to honor her achievement. We rented a couple of cabins on the shore of a nearby lake, and for two or three days around Alita's graduation we were able to visit, enjoy some leisure time, and get ready for the big celebration. The day she walked across the stage we hooted and hollered in a manner appropriate to higher education, took lots of pictures, then went back to the cabin for a celebration feast.

Throughout the evening meal, we focused on Alita's achievement, her collegiate experience, and what the future might hold.

As we cleared away the dinner dishes, the family moved into the living room to continue visiting and celebrating. As usual, my mom and dad stayed quietly out of the limelight, allowing their rambunctious kids and their young families to joke, tease, and enjoy being together. Still, I could see in my parents' proud smiles and gleaming eyes the joy and satisfaction they were deriving from this reunion.

I wondered at the time how much significance Mom and Dad had attached to this milestone. You see, I have two brothers in addition to my sister. Eleven years separate oldest from youngest, and all four of us happened to go to college. That means that for thirteen years out of a fifteen-year span, my parents were helping to pay at least one kid's tuition bill, and for eight of those years they were paying on two bills.

It had always been my parents' goal to be able to send their kids to college if they chose to go. Our family tree is full of teachers and preachers, and higher education has always been considered a priority. Of course, teachers and preachers aren't the highest paid occupations in the world, and so in our family education's high priority was always somewhat in tension against its high cost. For my parents to consider sending four kids through college was no small commitment on their part. I wondered as I sat in that lakeside cabin's living room if my parents had yet realized what a milestone they had just passed.

All four of us kids wanted them to realize it. That's why we did what we did. Some of us went to get the cake, some of us went to get cameras, and some of us went to get "the album." Pulling Mom and Dad gently from the outer edge of the crowd into the limelight, we shifted gears from celebrating my sister's accomplishment to celebrating my parents' accomplishment.

Before them we laid dessert—a huge cake decorated with the simple words, "Thanks, Mom and Dad, for college." Then we presented them with the album we had assembled a few weeks in advance. Inside, the book of memories began with a photo of all four of us when my sister was about one and my oldest brother was about twelve. In that photo, the three boys all had matching red and white pajamas, and the little girl who had just walked across the stage that afternoon looked like a baby princess.

As Mom and Dad paged tearfully through the book, they found personal letters of gratitude from each of us, photographs from our respective college days, and a photocopy of each of our college diplomas. At the end was a current picture of their four kids, the boys now all over six feet tall and the girl full grown as well. The contrast between the opening pajama picture and the final shot of four college graduates was remarkable and moving. And so were the values and sacrifices that had put those four kids through college.

Time Will Tell

That happy graduation weekend, it was entirely appropriate for us to celebrate the specific events of the day. It was also fitting that we commemorate the past four years of work and accomplishment my sister had just completed. But something else needed to be acknowledged as well, something that went beyond any of the four kids' achievements or even that of my parents. We needed to acknowledge the common values we shared as a family.

We had chosen four different majors, at four different schools, leading to four different career paths. But we had all chosen education as a priority. We had all chosen to work hard and make sacrifices to reach the graduation platform. And now we all chose to salute one of the values that held us together as a family, and to salute the parents who had instilled those values.

The values we were celebrating with that album are the kind of values the man in us chooses to champion—values that prove themselves to be worthwhile over time. The man in us tells us that what's truly important often lies beyond our immediate grasp or view. Our values need to be driven by faith and vision, not yielded to temporal pleasure or convenience.

This man in us who believes the eventual is important is the same one who makes decisions based on principles and who exercises caution in his personal disciplines. He has the capacity to look beyond the horizon of today and base his values on the promised outcomes of tomorrow.

The Farsighted Jerk in Us

There's a difference between being foresighted and being far-sighted, and that difference separates the man in us from the jerk in us in the arena of values. To be foresighted implies that you're existing in the present but able to take the future into account. To be farsighted implies that you can't see what's right in front of your face.

The jerk in us avoids today as passionately as the brat in us avoids tomorrow. His focus on the future is really just an excuse for neglecting action or responsibility in the present. The jerk in us tells us not to rush into anything, because the situation is likely to change tomorrow. He advises us to get more training, or give it more thought, or ask for more advice, or do more research, all with the supposed hope that future problems can be avoided. The problem, of course, is that ultimately our control over the future is extremely limited, and the jerk in us would have us wait until that control can be absolute.

In the meantime, he worries. That's the specialty of the jerk in us. He's preoccupied with future consequences, but he can't do much about them, so he sits and wrings his hands in fear. This is particularly tragic in the arena of values, because the jerk in us will tell us that what's truly important is based on so many contingencies that none of them can be meaningfully addressed right now. So while he prophetically points to tomorrow, he apathetically retreats from today as temporal and unimportant.

The jerk in us also gives us permission to procrastinate. He tells us not to take that family vacation because a recession might be brewing. He tells us not to start sharing our faith because we need more training. He tells us not to take the first step in a relationship because the other person might make the first move tomorrow. At key times of value judgment, the jerk in us can pull out the biggest lie in his arsenal. He'll merely tell us that the time to act is later.

Moving the Big Swingset

A few days after writing these words, we will be moving across town to a different house. Getting ready to move has been quite an experience, and has forced many value judgments between the importance of the immediate and the importance of the eventual. One of the biggest value judgments has been over moving our kids' huge swingset.

Actually, the word swingset doesn't do it justice. It's one of those lumber monstrosities that you buy at the hardware store as a "kit," before you realize how broadly some people define the word. Our "kit" took me and four of my probably former friends a day and a half to build, using tools that only a skilled craftsman knows how to use. Of course, the most complicated thing I've ever built with my own hands is a backyard compost bin, so I may be overstating the project's complexity a little.

Anyway, I figured when we sold our house, the swingset would stay with it. My wife figured otherwise. Once we discovered our divergent understandings, a values discussion ensued. I insisted that the structure had limited long-term value. She insisted that its immediate value was monumental. I asked her if it was really worth the trouble to move. She asked me if I had four other friends and a master craftsman who would help me build another one at the new house.

For days we fretted over that swingset. She fretted over my reluctance to take it. I fretted over her reluctance to leave it behind. We both fretted over how to solve the problem.

From my perspective, the jerk in me was having his way. The problem remained in the future. Our relationship was suffering in the present. That which was really important today had been subjugated to that which was relatively unimportant tomorrow.

The jerk in me got booted out when we decided that one way or another, the swingset was important enough to move and our relationship was too important to continue fretting. With the help of a dear friend, the swingset has been partially disassembled, and four other dear friends are going to try and help me pry the remaining structure out of the frozen January ground. We're doing what we can today with a view toward moving day, and we'll see what happens.

Balancing the Man

The man in us helps us to see beyond that which is immediate and to base our values on that which is ultimate. He knows that good things come to those who wait, and that postponing pleasure or satisfaction for higher good is a hallmark of maturity. The man in us helps us make better long-term decisions and maintain patience in our discipline, because he's a distance runner, not a sprinter. His head is up, his breathing is paced, and his eyes are on the finish line, not the grueling track at our feet.

But we can't let our values be based only on the eventual. We can't ignore what's important today just because something might change tomorrow. Some things have to be important today even if embracing them brings difficulty tomorrow. If our life is going to be based on a solid set of values, we have to learn to embrace today with a prudent awareness of tomorrow. Forging out that balance between the importance of the immediate and the importance of the eventual requires that our values be governed by the important character trait of discernment.

EMBRACING TODAY

In an Eternal Way

DISCERNMENT in Values:
The Immediate and the Eventual in the Balance

Every attitude and action that flows from our character into our daily lives can ultimately be traced back to our values. Our lives are regulated by that which we consider to be important or unimportant. That doesn't mean everything we think or do is deliberate. Lots of our values are formed by default. Sometimes in failing to choose what's really important, we yield to whatever outside people or forces are willing to choose for us.

As we form our values and seek to live by them, the boy in us can be a helpful advocate. He reminds us that today is the most significant day of our lives and that there are people and tasks which are immediately and legitimately important. He helps us find peace, even in troubled times, because he's so delightfully unconcerned with future woes. The boy in us urges us to view today as if it were the only day we had, and for some reason that approach does wonders in helping us decide what's truly valuable.

The man in us is equally helpful in forming and adhering to solid life values, because he reminds us that time does march on and that we live each today not only in the context of a yesterday and a tomorrow, but in the context of eternity. His heads-up vision allows us to time travel beyond today and imagine the consequences of our present course. If we like those consequences, we can stay the course. If not, we can return to today and change it.

The man in us can help give us an aerial view of our life, and in doing so help us plot better strategy and direction.

We need both the boy and the man in us to give us discernment in our values—to help us clearly see what's really important. While the boy in us tends to be nearsighted and the man in us farsighted, together they compensate for each other's weaknesses and help us to live each important day with an eye toward our ultimately important tomorrow.

Both the boy in us and the man in us can bring God's image into the arena of our values. The man in us brings a reflection of God's ability to transcend time and view things from an eternal perspective. The boy in us brings a reflection of the Yahweh "I AM" God who exists only in the eternal now. No wonder God's Word urges us to treasure both today and eternity. No wonder Jesus told us both to pray that God's kingdom would come and that to know it is already at hand.

Cleaning Out Grandma's House

My grandma was one of the most godly women I've ever known. When she died a couple of years ago at age eighty-eight, I never found a reason to shed a tear. I wouldn't have been embarrassed to cry for my own loss, or that of my family. But somehow the sadness of losing her from her frail body couldn't begin to eclipse the almost giggly joy I felt at her funeral. I've never been more sure of heaven or more assured of my own salvation than during those days when we eulogized her life—and cleaned out her house.

It's amazing how clearly a person's life and values can be summarized by what they leave behind. Grandma had lived alone since my grandpa had died twenty-five years earlier, and there was a lot of stuff packed into her little house. As we began the laborious task of sifting and stacking, we basically sorted her belongings into four categories. When we were finished, I realized that these four categories did more than represent the values of Grandma's life. One day they will represent and measure the values of my life, and yours.

Category One: Immediate Junk

We all have our eccentricities, and I guess elderly people are entitled to more of them than the rest of us. Throughout Grandma's house we found stuff we couldn't imagine anyone choosing to keep. Her attic had a pull-down ladder in the hallway, and at the top of that ladder were piles of randomly strewn junk. It was clear from the position of the stacks that Grandma probably just stood at the bottom of the ladder and threw this stuff up into the black hole where she could no longer climb.

It was actually kind of funny to picture Grandma pulling down that ladder and playing basketball in her hallway. Even funnier was the stuff she had chosen to toss up instead of out. There were dress patterns from the 1940s and 1950s, newspapers and magazines, old hats and clothes, and boxes of receipts that had long outlasted the products for which they vouched. Most of the stuff appeared to have been there for anywhere from a few months to a few years. Though she had once given it at least some value, it was now immediate junk. We threw it away as fast as we could scoop it up and carry it out.

Category Two: Eventual Junk

Some of the belongings we carried out of Grandma's house were what I'd call eventual junk. They consisted of old furniture, mattresses, dishes, pots and pans, clothing—things that she legitimately needed while she was living, but now that she was gone, held no value to any of us.

The furniture was kind of scratched up from the cats Grandma had adopted over the years. Many of the dishes and kitchen utensils hadn't been touched for a long time. The few plates, bowls, and spoons in the dish rack were all Grandma needed when we weren't there.

We couldn't help but smile as we disassembled Grandma's "souped up" bed. To treat one of her ailments the doctor had suggested elevating the head of her bed. It was a full twelve inches higher than the foot, and Beth and I laughed again remembering the one time we had slept in it and spent the whole night clawing our way back up the steep incline.

At one time, all of these things had served Grandma well, but time had diminished their value considerably. We called a local church who has a ministry to poor and homeless people, and they sent a couple of guys over in a pickup truck to haul it away. Even though it was raining, they didn't seem concerned with protecting their marginally valuable cargo. There's not a lot of difference between immediate junk and eventual junk—a couple of years at the most.

Category Three: Immediate Treasure

Amidst the immediate junk and eventual junk, however, were caches of genuine treasure. Photographs, letters, significant newspaper clippings—it was clear that much of Grandma's attention and values had centered on people, especially her family and her church. Grandma was energized by the people in her life. The year before her death, Grandma's dear next-door neighbor who looked in on her regularly would sometimes write my dad to tell him that Grandma wasn't getting dressed every day or didn't seem to be eating enough. Yet whenever any of us went to visit, Grandma had her hair done, her best dress on, and our favorite desserts baked.

Because of how highly she prized the people in her life, Grandma loved pictures, and she especially loved getting up-to-date photographs of grandchildren and great-grandchildren. In her latter days, she had been physically unable to frame the photos we sent or display them attractively in an album. But beside the big chair where she sat to watch television, they were scotch-taped directly to the wall.

Actually, the last several times we had visited Grandma she had started bequeathing photographs and other treasures to us a few at a time. I smiled as I entered her guest bedroom and saw the solitary boyhood picture of my dad hanging on top of two obviously empty spaces and nail holes in the wall. For years there had been a grouping of three black-and-white portraits there—my dad, my older brother and me, all as boys. One of the last times we visited Grandma, she had led me into this room and pulled my picture off the wall to give to me. My brother said she had done the same with him. Both of us had urged her to leave them there, reminding her we could always get them from her later if she wanted. But Grandma had insisted, noting that she didn't know how much longer she'd be able to give us things personally. Now we took down the remaining picture of my dad and placed it carefully in the box of immediate treasures we would take out of her little home and into ours.

Category Four: Eventual Treasure

As we sorted through Grandma's books, magazines, and papers, we soon needed to start a stack in the corner just for Bibles and one just for devotional reading material. There was an incredible abundance of both. When everything had been sorted, the stack of thin devotional magazines and books was almost as tall as the stack of twenty-seven Bibles. Together they were taller than I was, and I remember thinking at the time that what they represented in Grandma's life deserved to stand much taller than me.

Grandma had been a faithful member of the same church for over sixty years. She had taught Sunday school classes of various ages, and rarely missed a service. She had led my dad to Christ when he was a small boy, and my dad had led me to Christ at a similar age. Grandma told us that she prayed for us daily, and I knew that she did. There's nothing I miss more about her than her faithful intercession.

I know that Grandma's Bibles belonged in the category of immediate treasure to her while she was alive. But in those days immediately following her death, they symbolized for me an entirely new category—the category of eventual treasure. In my life, I knew I only saw through a glass darkly what she now sees face-to-face. I knew that her entire life had been built on values that honored God and served people. Now Grandma was enjoying the eventual treasure on which her hope had been built each and every immediate day of her life. And each time my gaze fell on that stack of Bibles, I promised again that my hope would be built on nothing less.

Taking Time to Clean House

Maybe it's an oversimplification to say that all of life's values can fall into four categories. Maybe not. It's certainly true that each of us is filling our little house with real and perceived treasure, and with junk.

Some of the treasure is immediate. We invest in it and enjoy it right now. This immediate treasure has to do with our relationships, with the people around us whose eternal nature makes them intrinsically important. We carried immediate treasure out of Grandma's house because it had value beyond her life. More than just photographs and memories, we drew from Grandma's life her character, her commitments, her values, her love, and her service to others. This kind of treasure is created and enjoyed immediately, but it is treasure because it doesn't pass away with time.

Of course, some of the junk in our lives is eventual. By that I mean it has some lingering usefulness. There are physical necessities in our lives, and we'd be foolish to deny or ignore them. Some junk is worth working for and having, at least for a while, and it's not wrong to value some eventual junk. But to qualify as eventual junk, the junk has to serve people. The homes we buy, the cars we drive, the food we eat, the music we listen to, the things we read—all can help us to lay up both immediate and eventual treasure. It's only when our junk starts to replace our treasure that we need to inventory our house and remind ourselves that, in the end, it's still junk.

The immediate junk, in my opinion, is the most dangerous. It's not just that the immediate junk has the least value, it's that it can so easily masquerade as eventual junk, and even as treasure. Our eventual junk is the basic material things of life that everyone wants and that aren't that hard to come by. But our immediate junk is where we can differentiate ourselves from others. We can work hard to accumulate bigger or better or more precious or more impressive stuff, and in doing so prove ourselves "better" than those around us. In the process, we want to earn a better position, achieve a higher education, make a better salary, raise a more privileged kid—and all of a sudden the immediate junk has replaced the treasure. We catch ourselves furiously throwing things up into a black hole that never seems satisfied, and never seems full. Meanwhile our relationships suffer, and our souls are empty, because we've chosen to invest in the wrong category.

Simply put, demonstrating maturity in the critical life arena of values requires the important character trait of discernment. All of us are going to fill our houses with junk and treasure, both immediate and eventual. A character with discernment, however, will help us keep the categories separate and the right stacks growing. The key stack to build upon is eventual treasure, and the key stack to purge is immediate junk. Values based on the reverse of that tend to turn the rest of our character upside down.

It took a lifetime for Grandma to carry all that stuff into her house. It only took us a couple of days to clear it all out. How quickly our life values can be evaluated by others when we let them inside our little house.

Jesus and Values

Some of the most pointed things Jesus said were about discerning what's really important. His Sermon on the Mount took the prevailing values of the day and turned them upside down. His confrontations with the Pharisees took their hypocritical religious values and turned them inside out. His parable about the prodigal son taught that a loving Father waits for us to recognize the immediate junk of pig food and return to the immediate and eventual treasure of being a son.

Jesus left nothing mystical or hidden in His statements about values. When He was asked which commandment was most important, He said love God with your whole being and love others as yourself. When Martha found herself preparing a big meal alone and asked Jesus about Mary's values, He replied that Mary had discerned the most important thing, and it was time with Him.

At every turn, Jesus was setting aright values that had been toppled and distorted. Selfish man has an incredible capacity to discard treasure in favor of junk, and to choose the worthless over the valuable. This was clear in Jesus' words, but even clearer in His very person and mission. For the stone which the builders rejected has become the cornerstone. And we would be wise to build our lives on its incredible value.

Work and play, decisions, discipline, communication, relationships, priorities, motives, and now values—we've come a long way toward the heart and core of our character. But even more foundational and pivotal to our character development than the values on which we build our lives is the point of view from which those values are created. At the center of our character, we find the arena of perspective.

Don't Just Take My Word for It

Valuing the immediate can be good:

> *Now listen to me, you that say, "Today or tomorrow we will travel to a certain city, where we will stay a year and go into business and make a lot of money." You don't even know what your life tomorrow will be! You are like a puff of smoke, which appears for a moment and then disappears. What you should say is this: "If the Lord is willing, we will live and do this or that."* (James 4:13–15)

———

Living only for the moment is bad:

> *Some will use gold or silver or precious stones in building on the foundation; others will use wood or grass or straw. And the quality of each person's work will be seen when the Day of Christ exposes it. For on that Day fire will reveal everyone's work; the fire will test it and show its real quality.* (1 Corinthians 3:13)

———

Valuing the eventual can be good:

> *To have faith is to be sure of the things we hope for, to be certain of the things we cannot see. . . . It was faith that made Moses, when he had grown up, refuse to be called the son of the king's daughter. He preferred to suffer with God's people rather than enjoy sin for a little while. He reckoned that to suffer scorn for Messiah was worth far more than all the treasures of Egypt, for he kept his eyes on the future reward.* (Hebrews 11:1, 24–36)

———

Living only for the future is bad:

> *So do not worry about tomorrow; it will have enough worries of its own. There is no need to add to the troubles each day brings.* (Matthew 6:34)

Discernment balances the value of the immediate with the value of the eventual:

> *Jesus Christ is the same yesterday, today, and for ever.* (Hebrews 13:8)

Character Trait #9

Wisdom

in Perspective

...understanding
your PLACE
in the concept
of GRACE

THE EYES HAVE IT

Thursdays were always my favorite day of basketball practice. Early in the week, our coaches had dastardly things on their minds, like wind sprints for conditioning or punishing lectures about last week's game. But by Thursday everyone, including the coaches, was getting pumped up for the big game on Friday night. All was forgiven from the previous week, and we were ready to take on the next challenging opponent.

Thursdays were our beloved "light workout." We talked strategy, worked on our offense, and shot free throws. But we didn't run too hard or do anything too strenuous, because if there was anything the coaches didn't want to happen on Thursday, it was an injury. Injuries on Mondays could mend by Friday night. Injuries on Thursdays could lose ball games.

On this particular Thursday, a jovial atmosphere dominated the locker room after practice. The workout had been easy, the coaches had been in a particularly good mood, and tomorrow night's opponent was one we had a good chance of defeating. Laughter, towel-snapping, soap-throwing—we were enjoying locker room frolic at its best.

My buddy Bill was one of the team's biggest cut-ups. He was always horsing around, always doing something to your locker or gym bag, always staying one up on you. It never did any good to retaliate against Bill, because he was always willing to take it one step further.

But that Thursday I had bested Bill. I had entered the showers before him, and in some kind of good-natured interchange he had ended up throwing a bar of soap at me. In returning his fire, I had been right on the money. Bill had to duck quickly, and the slippery, sudsy bar of soap went straight through the air where his head had been and into his open locker. His pants were hanging by one belt loop with the waist wide open, and my three-point soap shot stuck only momentarily against the inside of his back pocket before slithering down the leg and into Bill's open shoe. The cheer that went up from the other guys rivaled anything I had heard at the previous week's game.

Bill seemed to take it well. I had cleaned his clock, as well as the inside of his pants, and he knew it. As I stood there in the shower rinsing my hair, I had a feeling Friday night's game was going to be a good one. A shot like the one I just made had to be an omen of things to come.

Peek-a-Boo Problems

When someone tapped me on the shoulder, I turned to face them, wiping the water clear of my eyes and looking up to see who was going to congratulate me on my timely Bill payment. Then everything went dark. And the pain was tremendous.

I found out later that Bill's weapon had been an empty—make that almost empty—tube of shampoo. Having filled it with water, Bill had sneaked up behind me and then squirted the tube in my face when I turned. Apparently there was still some soap left in the tube, and Bill's direct hit in my right eye brought an instant and excruciating burning sensation.

Instantly, Bill knew he had made a big mistake and began apologizing profusely. For several minutes I stood there trying to rinse my eye out in the shower. But the burning continued, and try as I might, I couldn't open that eye for more than a second before the discomfort became unbearable. Bill helped me out of the shower and to the trainer's office, still apologizing and repenting of every practical joke he had ever played. The trainer gave me an eye-wash solution and gave Bill a severe tongue-lashing. After several minutes of using the solution and finding only minimal relief, the trainer sent me home with the bottle.

Doctor Stand-Up Takes a Look

That night was without a doubt the single most painful night of my life. Apparently your eye is one of the most sensitive parts of your body, and there was no escaping the pain. After tossing and turning all night, that tough seventeen-year-old varsity player finally broke down into tears. The next morning, my dad took me to the hospital emergency room.

As the doctor was rinsing my eye out with a little hose, he called out the brand name of the shampoo that Bill had used. I was amazed. How did he know what kind of shampoo it had been? It wasn't that difficult, he replied, there was so much soap in my eye that it was still "lathering" as he rinsed it, and he recognized the smell. He also asked if I wanted a cream rinse. I was barely amused. It was a brand of shampoo, he continued, that was noted for its high detergent content and potential for irritation. Nice choice, Bill.

I told the doctor that tonight was game night, and asked him if I'd still be able to play. He wanted to know where the game was, and I asked him what difference that made. "Oh, none," he replied, but he might want to come watch. He'd never seen anyone play without any depth perception, and it could be kind of funny. Have you ever noticed there are no doctors-turned-comedians?

But the doc was right. With one eye covered, I was having trouble discerning how far away things were. He fixed me up with an eye patch, and told me that about eighty percent of my cornea (the clear outer layer protecting the eye ball) had been damaged by the abrasive shampoo. Over time it would heal and grow back, but for now my vision would be about 20/80.

Trying to Make Up the Difference

It's probably a testimony to how weak our team was that year that my coaches chose to still let me start the game that night with my eye patch. And I've never been able to escape the irony that we played a team named the Pirates. I still think they thought the whole eye-patch thing was a put-on to try and psych them out. Unfortunately, it only seemed to make them angrier. The team that we should have beaten handily that night came out blazing. They handed us an embarrassing defeat, and afterwards one of their cheerleaders asked me if I'd consider being their back-up mascot.

Everyone should try playing basketball with an eye patch sometime. I had never realized how important having two eyes a couple of inches apart is to normal vision. If you've never done it before, shut one eye and have someone hold their two index fingers up, one about six inches closer than the other. Being able to discern how far away things are depends heavily on having two perspectives, one from each eye.

I still remember the pass I threw to Bill on a breakaway that night. I thought he was much farther away. It cleared his outstretched arms by about ten feet, and went sailing off the court toward our bench. Fortunately, our head coach leaped to his feet and kept the pass from going into the crowd. Well, maybe "fortunately" isn't the right word. I still remember the odd, frustrated face he made at me, then toward heaven. But for some reason he threw the ball back in to Bill. It had quite a bit of steam on it as I recall.

Because I knew I was handicapping the team, I probably tried too hard that night. The team needed my regular scoring contribution, and I was trying to make a lot of stuff happen that my limited perspective just wouldn't allow. As it turned out, I only made one outside shot that night. It was about a twenty-five footer from out past the top of the key, but it drew more jeers than cheers. I guess they'd never seen many shots banked off the backboard from out there before.

Different Points of View: The Critical Need for Perspective

Much more important than the basketball part of that story is the perspective part. Perspective refers to our point of view. Perspective is necessary in order to perceive and understand something's depth and complexity. When you have a good perspective, you see things as they really are because you see them multidimensionally. One point of view is almost always flawed. Two or more points of view insure a much more reliable picture.

Especially when something has many parts or aspects, you need perspective to be able to accurately relate the parts to each other, and to the whole. I can't think of a better word to describe the innermost arena of a guy's character.

Deep inside, each one of us has our own view of ourselves and the world around us. It's a view that's been colored and influenced by many factors over the years, some of them well beyond our own ability to recognize or understand. If we're tilted toward brat or jerk in other arenas, it's usually here in the perspective arena that the excess finds its root.

It's from the core arena of perspective that a guy builds his basic values, his determination of what's important and what's not. From those values flow his motives, the reasons "why" he thinks the things he thinks, says the things he says, and does the things he does. In this inner core of a guy's character, the trinity of perspective, values, and motives rule the inner life and set the tone for what will happen in the other, more visible character arenas.

If we intend to have any real control over our own characters, or any power to change the things we don't like, we have to be willing to explore this inner arena of our personal perspective. The boy in us is ready to help. He's the part of us that perceives our own personal significance, and urges us to give incredible value to who we are.

"AREN'T I GOOD?"

The boy in us has a perspective that perceives our significance

Have you ever wondered why everyone talks about the notorious "male ego," but never about a corresponding "female ego"? Probably not, because even we guys admit how much we like to feel good about ourselves. It's not that our female counterparts don't have egos. They're just pitifully dwarfed by comparison to ours.

We guys seem to have an innate need to win, to be right, and to be admired, especially in relationship to the women in our lives. Chauvinistic? Absolutely. Superiority complex? You bet. Any chance of reform? Well, lots of us are working on it with varying degrees of success.

In the meantime, the women around us have this male ego of ours to deal with. They can ignore it, but that just makes it worse because then we just start doing pathetic things to cry out for their attention. They can feed it, but that just makes us more cocky and annoying, especially to onlooking women who don't love us as much and don't understand that even ugly, primitive animals deserve to be fed occasionally. Or they can do what most women do with their loved ones' male egos. They can feed us a healthy diet of praise and respect, and slap us up the side of the head when we get too obnoxious for our own good.

A Tie Goes to the Husband

Early in our marriage, Beth and I instituted a policy that has led us through countless impasses and kept my male ego fed without being gorged. The policy is simply called "a tie goes to the husband."

"A tie goes to the husband" has nothing to do with neckwear, and very little to do with baseball. It is, however, rooted in the baseball regulation that says when a runner's foot reaches the base at the same time as the ball reaches the fielder covering that base, a tie goes to the runner. It's a rule that acknowledges how difficult it is to reach base in the first place, and how perilous it is trying to stay there once you've arrived.

I don't know about you, but when it comes to my need to win, be right, and feel admired by my wife, I need every concession I can get. When we were younger, I had a lot less trouble winning over Beth. In games like tennis, volleyball, or racquetball I was far superior. But as time has passed, the games at which we compete are not nearly so slanted in my favor. Now we play things like board games or card games or word games—all based more on knowledge, memory, finesse, or strategy than physical strength. Where did my advantage go? She sometimes beats me even in miniature golf!

And if winning has become harder, how about being right? It sure seems like I was right a lot more before I got married. Now Beth remembers more details, knows more names, intuits more directions, and recalls the precise location of every item in our house that I pronounce to be missing or lost.

Now I ask you, how am I supposed to feel admired by my wife when she's doing more than her share of the winning and being right? That's where our "a tie goes to the husband" rule may be saving our marriage, or at least salvaging my male ego. In "a tie goes to the husband," the understanding is that if I can work the contest or question of who's right to a tie or state of inconclusiveness, we declare me the winner.

One day Beth and I were trying to think of the last name of an acquaintance we had known in college. After some thought, she insisted she knew the name. It didn't sound familiar to me, so I told her that wasn't it. Sensitive as always to my compulsion for being right, she went to look for a college directory of some kind. She couldn't find one—which in itself, boosted my ego since she can always find everything—and I was able to declare, "a tie goes to the husband!" If we couldn't prove me wrong, I was right.

I wish I had let it go there. But she had been winning a lot lately, and had certainly been right more than fifty percent of the time. So I rubbed it in a little. I told her it was too bad we hadn't bet on it. I would have been willing to bet a million dollars that the name she thought of wasn't correct. It was a good thing I had been compassionate with her fading memory, I gloated, or she might be working off a big debt now.

Unfortunately, this must have qualified as one of those male ego displays that deserved a slap up side of the head rather than tender, loving admiration. Beth took my hand, shook it, and bet me a million dollars. Then she went on a tireless crusade to find that college directory. A couple of days later, after she had dragged me through the reorganization of every closet and file in our house, we found a college directory that listed the name we had been trying to remember. And the husband who had just barely tied his way on to first base was thrown out by a mile trying for second. Actually, it was more like a million miles.

The Right to Remain Right

The boy in us needs to win, needs to be right, needs to be admired. He's the confident, self-assured aggressive part of us that reminds us we're unique, valuable, gifted, and capable of making a meaningful contribution to our world. The boy in us perceives his own significance and convinces us never to sell ourselves short. He has a high confidence in what he can do and has the drive to do it. When he's knocked down he never stays down. He believes in himself and expects others to believe in him too.

The perspective of the boy in us is that we are responsible for our life, and that our only limitations are self-imposed. We have great potential to impact the world for good, and a great responsibility to live up to that potential.

The boy in us brings his work proudly to the teacher's or the employer's desk and boldly asks them to praise it or help him improve it. He makes decisions with confidence and pursues his personal disciplines with tenacity. He's persuasive and compelling in his communication, and in his relationships he earns the confidence and admiration of those he loves and those he leads. He's willing to trust people, to believe in them and depend on them, because he expects others to hold themselves to the same high standards he does.

Because the boy in us perceives his own significance and has a high view of his ability to make an impact, his values are idealistic and visionary. The motives that flow from those values are commendable and largely transparent. He's on a crusade to champion noble causes and build a life of significance. The boy in us won't let us settle for mediocrity in our perspective, because he wants our life to count for something, hopefully something big.

The Conceited Brat in Us

The potential problem with a high perception of our own significance, of course, is that our perception will be too high and that our dependency on our own abilities and efforts will grow too strong. When that happens, the conceited brat in us is vying for control of our perspective.

The brat in us is more than aware of his own significance, he's preoccupied and enamored with it. He can take us quickly from self-reliance to self-sufficiency to self-absorption. When the brat in us is in control, we can drift from a healthy, positive view of ourselves into a lofty, exalted view of self at the center of our life and even the center of our universe. And there's no perspective that's more distorted or dangerous for us than the one at the center of our universe, because only One deserves that place of honor.

Whether he realizes it or not, the brat in us is embracing a perspective that says we don't need God. We can stand on our own. No one is more important than ourselves. And from that distorted perspective can flow an entire character of distorted values and motives that can pollute every arena of our lives.

Digging Through Rhonda's Purse

I remember sitting in the bleacher seats of our junior high gym and wondering if Judy liked me. She probably did, I thought. After all, I liked her. We were of comparable social status. The relationship would be good for both of us, not to mention enjoyable. So why hadn't she replied yet to my proposal to go steady? There was probably something brewing between her and her friends. They must have been playing some cat-and-mouse game and crafting some strategic response to make her seem more desirable. Remember how a junior high boy's mind works?

Judy's friend, Rhonda, had been sitting nearby, and I noticed it when she left her seat to go talk to someone. Rhonda was the one who was supposed to have posed the going steady question to Judy for me, but no reply had come from her yet. She had been gone from her seat for several minutes, and knowing how Rhonda could talk, she'd probably be gone several minutes more. That's when my eyes fell on her purse.

I knew that junior high girls communicate frequently by passing notes, and that important notes were indigenous to their purses. I mentioned that observation to my buddy, and in a flash he had grabbed her purse and handed it to me. Rhonda was now nowhere in sight.

For the next few minutes, my buddy and I had a blast. There was no note about Judy in there, but it was full of other amusing treasures. We laughed and teased about each embarrassing item we found, reading the notes that were none of our business and holding up some of the girl stuff for the hoots they prompted from the other juveniles around us. Just as I got to the bottom of the bag, I looked up into Rhonda's fuming face. She repossessed her violated purse with an angry snatch, and furiously jammed the contents back inside without saying a word. She didn't really have to, though.

My partner in crime scoffed at Rhonda's indignation, and pretended she had taken our "joke" too seriously. After he walked away, I sat there for a few minutes, embarrassed and humiliated in my own conscience. What had I been thinking? What right did I have to invade her purse and make public display of her private stuff? How would I have felt if she had emptied my wallet or gym bag in the same way?

I didn't have good answers to those questions back then, but in retrospect I see that one conceited junior high brat had let his self-absorption turn him into someone he didn't really want to be. I had allowed my agenda, my own sense of self-importance, my conceited impatience to get the answer I wanted lead me to violate someone else's territory.

The brat in me still lets that kind of thing happen. When my perspective is that my agenda is most important, that my wants should govern my values, motives, relationships, decisions—in short that self is sovereign—then that perspective is always going to lead me unhesitatingly into someone else's purse. Ultimately it will lead me into God's purse, into His rightful possession of my life. And the brat in me can never help me get used to the fury I find in God's eyes when I realize I've violated His place of sovereign lordship in my life.

Balancing the Boy

At his best, the boy in us coaches a healthy self-image and an accurate, positive view of our uniqueness as individuals. He gives us confidence in ourselves, and challenges us to take responsibility for our lives. The boy in us is used to relying on his own efforts, and has enjoyed considerable success in doing so. He personifies the best the human spirit has to offer.

At his worst, the brat in us tells us we deserve to be at the center of our values and at the top of our priority list. He elevates our self-sufficiency to idol status, and subtly communicates that we can feel good about ourselves in the power of our own strength. The brat in us puts self at the center instead of God, and that perspective is distorted and destructive, both to ourselves and those around us. That's why perceiving our own significance needs to be balanced with perceiving our own insignificance, and this is the vantage point which the man in us brings to our perspective.

"I'M UNWORTHY"

The man in us has a perspective that perceives our insignificance

A few weeks after a recent election, an article in a news magazine caught my eye. There were several black-and-white photos of historical-looking men, and the contrast between them and the rest of the colorful magazine made me curious. The article started by listing eight or ten obscure names and asking me, the reader, if I could identify any of them. I couldn't. The names, along with the photos, seemed to represent anonymous, insignificant men undeserving of the space this major newsweekly had given them. Then the article revealed what each of those men had in common. They had each been Vice-President of the United States.

For some reason, that information really depressed me. The article's point was simply to illustrate what percentage of VP's go on to be President. But all I could think about was the fact that these were guys who had accomplished more than I was likely to accomplish in my lifetime, and who had attained a stature I had little hope of ever attaining. Yet a few years later, only history buffs and game-show hosts would have any idea who they were.

My mind began to wander to all the elite groups and lofty achievements that were beyond my reasonable grasp. There are lots of inner circles and upper echelons in countless fields of endeavor where a guy should be able to earn his place in history. Music, medicine, business, theology, entertainment, education—and many sub-categories within each—offered thousands of opportunities to be a household word. Yet I realized that my chances of infiltrating any of them, even temporarily, were less than remote. You could list my name in that article and even the historians and game-show hosts would be puzzled.

If there is a holy grail we guys universally pursue, it is probably best described as significance. How we define that word will vary greatly from person to person. Not everyone wants fame, fortune, or even to be noticed. But we all want our life to have some meaning, and for that meaning to be acknowledged by someone outside of ourselves. Obscurity we can live with. Insignificance is harder to swallow.

Then Sings My Soul

I don't have an outstanding singing voice. But our church is small, and if you have any musical ability at all you're encouraged, okay begged, to share it with the congregation in worship. A handful of us choir members typically rotate through a "special music" calendar that schedules us to sing once every couple of months.

On this particular Sunday, I had selected a simple praise chorus as my solo. In fact, it was so simple that it only had three verses and these were just minor variations such as "thank Him," "praise Him," and "love Him." I usually try to sing from memory, so the simple lyrics of this simple song had really put me at ease. As I stepped up to the microphone, I felt more confident and poised than ever before.

It made me think back to seventh-grade music class, and our eccentric and clueless music teacher who had required that each guy in class sing a solo during each grading period. It could be "Mary Had a Little Lamb" (and often it was), Handel's "Messiah," or the latest Beatles hit, but it had to be sung and it had to be solo. We all viewed this forced humiliation as cruel and unusual punishment at the time, but as I picked up the microphone that Sunday morning, I smiled at the thought of that seventh-grade music ordeal. I had come a long way since delivering "Raindrops Keep Fallin' on My Head" to a hostile group of juveniles.

The first couple of verses went fine. *"I will praise Him, . . . I will thank Him . . ."* —the tune was as simple as the words and I could relax and just sing the song. But I guess I relaxed too much. With my inhibitions about the song and the audience all but gone, I started thinking about the words I was singing. As the key change took me into the last verse of the song, the words remained simple, but turned personal. *"I will praise You, praise You, for You are worthy of praise . . ."* —and suddenly I couldn't sing any more. It was as if my heart expanded and rose into my throat. My eyes started burning as they welled up with tears, and my lower lip started trembling uncontrollably. Though I needed to swallow, I couldn't. As a matter of fact it's starting to happen to me now, just by writing about it.

I didn't know what to do. The pianist, a dear lady and my good friend, kept on playing softly, looking up at me with each new measure to see what I wanted to do. I couldn't do anything. I was falling apart. I had been gripped in my heart of hearts by God's worthiness to be praised, and by my unworthiness in His presence. No words were coming out, so I hastily put the microphone back in its stand and exited through a side door off of the platform. Sobbing in the hallway, I heard the pianist finish the song alone.

Me and the Boys in the Nursery

When my tears finally subsided, the reality of what had just happened started to hit me. The brat in me told me I had just made a fool of myself. The boy in me wondered if my leadership position in the church had been adversely affected—it certainly hadn't been a very confident, emotionally stable display. The man in me, however, was still running the show, and he needed to talk to someone about what had just happened. That's when I remembered that my wife was taking her turn in the nursery that Sunday. She didn't even know what had happened yet.

So I found my way through back hallways to the nursery, where Beth was kneeling among six or eight toddlers. A couple of them were crying, and I remember thinking, *Oh good, just what she needs, another crying boy.* So I perched on one of those tiny wooden chairs while she got the other kids happy. Then I explained to her why I wasn't in church.

I was surprised to see how calmly Beth received the news, given that people from the congregation would probably be arriving at any minute and asking her why her husband had an emotional breakdown in church. Her comforting words were that she was sure it had been fine, that people knew me and loved me and would accept the sincerity of the song's message, however it was delivered.

Then for the next several minutes, between wiping noses and helping children work puzzles, we discussed the overpowering reality of God's worthiness. In the end, we concluded that it shouldn't be that odd or unusual for God to humble one of His children in His presence. The odd or unusual thing is that it doesn't happen more often.

The Search for Insignificance

The man in us gives us an entirely different perspective on ourselves than the boy in us gives. If the boy in us brings us a perspective colored by idealism, the man in us brings a perspective colored by realism. He knows our limitations.

The man in us isn't afraid of obscurity, because he understands obscurity to be part of reality. Ninety-nine point nine percent of us will live lives of relative anonymity, and while the boy in us will give his all to beat those odds, the man in us submits to them. That doesn't make him unambitious or a quitter, however. While the man in us may accept his own obscurity, he still gives his all to find significance within it.

Perspective, according to the man in us, comes from outside ourselves. Only as we see ourselves as others see us can we have a truly objective view of our life and our character. Remember that the man in us also has values that favor the eventual over the immediate. He has motives based on what others expect from him rather than what he expects from others. Both of these come from a perspective that deliberately avoids being too subjective or too close to a situation to judge it accurately.

When we're listening to the man in us we can often avoid the pitfalls of arrogance and pride. We can step outside our own desires and goals long enough to see those others may have, and this gives us a much more responsible approach to our priorities, our relationships, and how we communicate. We treat others more compassionately, because our realistic perspective on ourselves frees us to see their significance rather than our own.

Even in the more public arenas of discipline, decisions, work and play, the man in us gives us a perspective that lets us say "no" to self-gratification and "yes" to things that require sacrifice or patience. Because he knows the universe doesn't revolve around him, he can help us work and play for the good of the group. He can help us make decisions that benefit everyone, not just himself. He can discipline himself to move toward goals that are significant rather than flashy. The man in us clears the way for all kinds of good, mature things to happen in our lives, because his perspective isn't blocked by the self-interest that is often our life's biggest stumbling block.

The Worthless Jerk in Us

To be obscure is not to be insignificant, and even to be insignificant is not to be worthless. As is so often the case in our character arenas, however, the jerk in us doesn't make those kinds of distinctions. Unlike the man in us who reminds us that our significance is relative to the whole, the jerk in us tells us that we are worthless, undeserving wretches who merit no one's favor, including God's.

I have a friend who sometimes seeks an escape from his wife's exhortations by declaring, "Oh, I'm just a worthless human being!" What can you demand of a guy who's just made that admission? Nothing! And that's precisely why the jerk in us declares our worthlessness to us over and over again. He's ready to be free of responsibility, free of change, free of character improvement and maturity. When our perspective becomes one that says we have no significance, no value, no worth, death is lurking at our spirit's door. There's no point in going on, no benefit to pressing forward.

The jerk's resignation from life is most tragic in the spiritual realm. While the brat in us dismisses God with the declaration that he doesn't need Him, the jerk in us dismisses God with the declaration that he doesn't deserve Him. And the most perilous of truths is that he's right.

The jerk in us beckons us to a perspective of worthlessness, because his view of our insignificance has slid into despair. From this inner despair, the jerk procrastinates, deceives, manipulates, and is distracted from meaningful character development. At the core of his being, he's dead, and his only hope lies in One who specializes in resurrection.

Balancing the Man

The man in us gives us the perspective that we live our life in a context. It's a context that includes history, a context that includes others, a context that includes eternity, and a context that includes an almighty God. By seeing our life and our self in those contexts, we can escape self-interest and perceive things more as they really are. We can cooperate better with the world around us, because we see things more objectively. The man in us is humbled by his own relative insignificance, and this humility can be a doorway to service and right relationship with others.

But we can't confuse obscurity with worthlessness. We can't abdicate our responsibilities or neglect our character out of a perspective that says we don't matter. Our perspective needs to be one that helps us understand our place in the context of God's overall plan, and one that acknowledges our significance from His point of view. At the innermost core of our being, our perspective must be kindred with God's, and the character trait He's provided for that purpose is wisdom.

UNDERSTANDING YOUR PLACE

In the Context of Grace

WISDOM in Perspective:
Significance and Insignificance in the Balance

Our inner perspective, like all our other character arenas, is being molded our whole life long. But our core arenas don't shift and change as easily as the outer arenas. To be more patient in our discipline is usually easier than being more humble in our relationships. And as hard as being more loving in our communication may be, positive change in that character arena is much easier than purifying our motives or discerning more eternal values. The closer you get to the center of your character, the more difficult change becomes.

It stands to reason, then, that the arena of our perspective is the most difficult and most critical of all. It's difficult because it runs the deepest. Often we don't understand why we act so conceitedly or feel so worthless. It's critical because even a minor change in our perspective can have incredible trickle-down effects on the rest of our character. For example, a small nudge from a conceited perspective to a more modest, but healthy, view of our significance could revolutionize our relationships. A slight drift from feeling insignificant to feeling worthless could lead us to decisions from which it would take a lifetime to recover.

The boy in us brings to our perspective a healthy self-concept, and there are few things more valuable in life. His perspective that we are capable and valuable and loved can give us a positive approach to life that can help us conquer our goals and overcome our adversities. The boy in us gives us our drive, our energy, our will to succeed. He's ambitious, smart, winsome, and determined. The world admires us most when the boy in us governs our perspective.

The man in us brings to our perspective a realism that usually outlasts and outperforms naive idealism. His perspective is that others are just as important as we are, if not more so, and that significance is found in emptying oneself out rather than filling oneself up. The man in us gives us our humility, our pragmatism, our willingness to cooperate. The man in us may not be a hero to the world, but he's almost always a hero to our family and friends. He's transcended obscurity by defining his own significance in the midst of historical insignificance. He's decided he's just as important as fifty percent of the vice-presidents in U.S. history.

We need both the boy in us and the man in us because, together, they can give us a perspective of wisdom. Wisdom is simply an accurate understanding of what is true and lasting. That which is true and lasting can only come from the One who is true and lasting, and so to embrace a right perspective on ourselves, we must embrace God's perspective on us. God agrees with the boy in us—we are significant because He created us and loves us. God agrees with the man in us—we are like grass that withers and fades away, insignificant except in relationship to Him.

Harvesting Tomatoes by Flashlight

Every year, Beth and I plant tomatoes in our garden. The Chicago area, where we live, doesn't have the longest growing season in the world, and every fall when the first frost threatens, we lament the fact that we didn't get the tomato plants out earlier in the spring. We always have lots of green tomatoes that die on the vine before they can ripen.

One frost-threatening October evening, the job fell to me to make one more trip to the garden and harvest anything with a remote chance of ripening inside. I was watching something on TV and let the time get away from me. All of a sudden it was 10 P.M. and I had forgotten to go to the garden.

It was already pretty chilly, so I quickly grabbed my jacket, a grocery bag, and the first flashlight I could lay my hands on. Out in the garden, I was quickly amazed at the ripening that had taken place. Just a couple of days earlier we had picked every tomato with a hint of color to it. Now tomato after tomato had a nice rosy glow to it.

I filled one grocery bag and went back to the house for another. Over an hour later, I returned to the house with nearly frozen fingers, a sore back, and the biggest single harvest of tomatoes our garden had ever produced. Beth stared in disbelief at the size of the bags, and started picking through the tomatoes to assess what I had done. They were all extremely green. Impossible! The moonlight hadn't been that good, but I had used a flashlight, and seen the ripe color with my own eyes.

"Is this the flashlight you used?" Beth asked with a knowing smile that was about to erupt into gleeful laughter. She held up my five-year-old's toy flashlight, the one that has three lenses: a clear one, a green one, and of course the one I had been using—the red one.

Using the Right Flashlight Lens

That night in the garden, the green lens would have brought the same result as the clear lens. Earlier in the year, the red lens would have been right at least part of the time. But only the clear lens could give me the right perspective all the time.

Of course if I could, I would have turned on the sun before I went outside that night. That would have made the job easier and given me better results. But absent that power, the clear lens was still my best hope for a right perspective.

How wonderful it would be if at the core of our character we could have a perspective that matched God's, one that "turns on the sun" and views our world and ourselves from a standpoint of what is true and lasting. While that perspective is not available in this lifetime, how fortunate we are that He at least offers us the option of a flashlight with a clear lens. That flashlight is a life perspective submitted to Him, and that clear lens is wisdom.

The Big Red Bandanna

My granddaddy is ninety-one now, and my grandmother is well into her eighties. They live in western Kentucky, about eight hours from our home (ten now that we have kids), and we usually can get down to see them only two or three times a year. We're grateful they can still live in their own home and do most things for themselves, but when news of severe weather or a robbery or something down there reaches us, we're always a little concerned.

That's why I was so glad to meet their friend Denny. Denny dropped by the house one summer afternoon when we were sitting in Grandmother's living room visiting. At first I thought how inconvenient it was that someone would drop in during our short family visit, but my grandparents both seemed delighted to see him and to introduce us to him. He came in and stayed awhile.

During the twenty minutes or so Denny was there, the conversation was pretty routine—the weather, farm prices, ailments of people they knew. It turned out Denny was a deacon in my grandparents' church, which surprised me since he appeared to be in his seventies himself. I was a deacon in my church at the time too, and I didn't see how someone his age could keep up with the many responsibilities that went with the job.

After a pleasant visit, Denny leaned forward in his chair and said he should be going, he just wanted to look in on my grandparents and make sure they were doing okay and had what they needed. Before he stood, though, my granddaddy asked Denny if he would lead us in prayer. Granddaddy never does good-nights or goodbyes without taking time for a devotional moment.

Denny kind of ducked his head and said, "Aw, Mr. Hooks, you know how I get." I had no idea what he meant, but my granddaddy (a.k.a. Mr. Hooks) must have because he replied that he knew what Denny meant, but it would mean a lot to him if he would pray for them before he left. Reluctantly, Denny agreed, and as I started to bow my head I saw him reach into his back pocket and quietly pull out a huge red bandanna. It was the kind you see more often in western Kentucky than in the suburban neighborhood where we live, the kind that a farmer wraps around his head on a hot summer day or ties around his finger when his work draws some blood.

Faded and worn at the edges, it was clear this red bandanna had been used faithfully for a long time.

Denny's prayer was short and direct, a few words of reverence and adoration for his heavenly Father and a simple request that God's grace would continue to minister to my grandparents' household. The prayer took a few minutes, though. Denny cried through every word of it. That's why he needed the red bandanna.

Afterwards, Denny left quietly with a warm smile and handshake for each of us, but no explanation for his outpouring of emotion. It had clearly been a moving experience for my grandparents as well. After a few moments of what felt like hallowed silence, they explained that ever since a significant event in Denny's life, he hadn't been able to come to God in prayer without weeping. He had asked to be excused from public prayers at church because he felt his emotion would be a distraction to others.

Those twenty minutes were the only ones I've ever spent with Denny, but from the moment he walked slowly out my grandparents' front door, I knew I wanted to be like him. Here was a man who accurately perceived his own significance. On a hot summer afternoon when most seventy-year-olds would have been home in a recliner, he had been out bringing comfort and blessing to two elderly saints who can't get out to church anymore. And he had given a certain young deacon a lifelong standard by which to measure his service to others.

Here, too, was a man who accurately perceived his own insignificance. A respected man in his community and a spiritual leader in his church, he still understood that great grace had entered his life, and he couldn't approach the Giver of that grace without tears of gratitude. In fact, to his credit, he didn't try. The same red bandanna that symbolized the sweat of his brow and the significant work of his life had also come to symbolize his continual brokenness before God, and the glory of insignificance in His presence. What perspective governed his life. What wisdom governed his perspective.

> The way to become wise is to honor the Lord; he gives sound judgment to all who obey his commands. He is to be praised for ever. (Psalm 111:10)

Putting It All in Perspective

At the very core of our character there are only two funda-mental perspectives: the foolish one that is self-centered and the wise one that is God-centered. Like me, you probably know all kinds of guys at all levels of maturity and character development. Some of them are slipping up because they're being too passionate in their decisions, too hurtful in their communication style, too preoccupied in their priorities. Others are showing great maturity because they're being patient in their discipline, humble in their relationships, pure in their motives. But all these victories or set-backs in character development are only as true and lasting as each person's inner perspective.

If the inner perspective of a guy's life is fundamentally foolish and self-centered, the maturing process of character development will always be frustrated, because the brat in him or the jerk in him will always be taking charge. Self at the center has an insatiable appetite. He has to be fed with things that make him feel worthy of his position, even though he's foolish for being there. When self is in the center, the brat in a guy is always grabbing, pushing, or pouting, because his conceited perspective is that he should have whatever he wants. The jerk in him is always bossing, manipulat-ing, or grumping around, because in his heart of hearts he senses his unworthiness for the position he has claimed for himself.

On the other hand, if the inner perspective of a guy's life is fun-damentally wise and God-centered, there will be consistent, steady growth toward maturity. Wisdom is not perfection, and even a guy who's steadily maturing will drift from side to side as the boy in him or the man in him exerts influence. But because the perspec-tive at the core of his being is God-centered, the character traits that demonstrate true maturity will be more and more evident each day of his yielded, faithful life.

Jesus and Perspective

What was the inner perspective of Jesus' character? John 13:3–5 says, "Jesus knew that the Father had given him complete power; he knew that he had come from God and was going to God.

So he rose from the table, took off his outer garment, and tied a towel round his waist. Then he poured some water into a basin and began to wash the disciples' feet and dry them with the towel around his waist."

Because Jesus knew His existence did not begin in Mary's womb nor end on Calvary's cross, He could embrace both the significance of being a savior, and the insignificance of being a servant. How amazing that the perfect perspective of God incarnate led Him to sacrifice and service! How inspiring that those who believe in Jesus can also know they have come from God and are going to God, and can build their characters on that same wise perspective!

Jesus' inner perspective was based on what is true and lasting. It was the perfect, wise perspective of God himself. And it made Jesus discerning in His values, pure in His motives, focused in His priorities, humble in His relationships, loving in His communication, patient in His discipline, responsible in His decisions, and creative in His work and play. It made him perfect in every character arena. And there is no other worthy standard for our character today than the perfect character of Jesus.

Don't Just Take My Word for It

Perceiving your significance is good:

But God in his grace chose me even before I was born, and called me to serve him. (Galatians 1:15)

———

Perceiving yourself as worthy is bad:

The LORD puts a curse on the homes of wicked men, but blesses the homes of the righteous. He has no use for conceited people, but shows favor to those who are humble. (Proverbs 3:33–34)

———

Perceiving your insignificance can be good:

> *But I reckon my own life to be worth nothing to me; I only want to complete my mission and finish the work that the Lord Jesus gave me to do, which is to declare the Good News about the grace of God.* (Acts 20:24)

———

Perceiving yourself as worthless is bad:

> *The LORD said to me, "I chose you before I gave you life, and before you were born I selected you to be a prophet to the nations." I answered, "Sovereign LORD, I don't know how to speak; I am too young." But the LORD said to me, "Do not say that you are too young, but go to the people I send you to, and tell them everything I command you to say. Do not be afraid of them, for I will be with you to protect you. I, the LORD, have spoken!"* (Jeremiah 1:4–8)

———

A wise perspective is one that balances my insignificance by myself with my significance in Christ:

> *When I look at the sky, which you have made, at the moon and the stars, which you set in their places—what is man, that you think of him, mere man, that you care for him? Yet you made him inferior only to yourself, you crowned him with glory and honor.* (Psalm 8:3–5)

CONCLUSION

Combining the Men and the Boys

Having walked through all nine character arenas, it might be fun to list them down one side of a sheet of paper, and then list the headings Boy, Brat, Man, Jerk across the top. Then, using the different criteria we've discussed, we could each do a character self-evaluation. Separating out the man in us from the boy in us can go a long way toward showing us our character flaws and weaknesses, as well as reinforcing the arenas where we're being successful and balanced.

But by the time we've made our nine X's in the thirty-six possible boxes, we might start feeling as if we have a multiple-personality disorder. Can all those guys really live inside us? Is it possible to let the brat in us dominate one arena and the jerk in us dominate another? Could we be pretty well balanced one day and then out of balance the next?

Of all the questions, like those our self-evaluation list might raise, probably none is more important than the question of how we might go about maturing our character in the arenas where we feel especially like a brat or a jerk. Yet it's hard to imagine waking up each day, pulling out our thirty-six-option character checklist, and taking inventory. No, this process of separating the men from the boys is more like a diagnostic exercise where you take all the pieces of an engine apart to better understand it. Eventually, you have to put it back together to see how it works. Now that we've separated the nine arenas—the boys, the brats, the men, and the jerks—let's pull them back together and think about one guy, with one character.

Cross-Country Caravaning

Probably the most ambitious youth trip I ever undertook during my youth ministry days started in the Chicago area, paused a couple of days to go whitewater rafting in West Virginia, then proceeded on to a camp in central Virginia. As we were planning the trip, a lot of the kids and sponsors really wanted to go to the ocean as well. So we decided that after the camp, we'd "swing by" Virginia Beach for a couple of days before heading back home.

Everything about that trip was underestimated. The number of kids who went, the number and types of vehicles we needed to get there, the amount of time it took to get from central Virginia to the coast—all seemed a lot smaller when we first planned the trip. Some groups might have simply arranged for a bus or two to transport sixty people across country. But we chose to have fourteen sponsors caravan in seven different vehicles ranging from a motor home to a Honda Accord.

On the way home, we had engine trouble with one of the vans and fell several hours behind. To make up the time, we were driving longer and later hours than we had originally intended. I was driving the lead vehicle, and trying to stay alert to the road before me while everyone else in our van slept. All seven vehicles had CB radios to help us communicate and stay together, but the air waves had been tranquilly silent for a couple of hours. I think everyone but the seven drivers was fast asleep.

Suddenly a penetrating, panicked female voice came in over the CB. "Good Lord, Nate, Ken's going to kill us all!" The alarm in her voice, along with the screeching volume and static over the radio, brought everyone vertical in our vehicle. The whole group wanted to know what was going on. So did I. That's when I looked in my side mirror and saw vehicle number three veering wildly from shoulder to shoulder on the two-lane highway.

Changing Drivers in Vehicle Number Three

I tried with the tone of my voice to bring a note of calmness back to the air waves as I quickly radioed the rest of the group to pull over. As soon as we were stopped, I jumped out and ran back to vehicle number three and its sleepy driver. Bending over to look inside, I saw Ken's smooshed face leaning against the driver's side window. He appeared to be using the emergency stop to catch a few Z's, and was totally unaware that his Z's were what had precipitated the stop in the first place.

I tapped on the window, and Ken looked up, then waved. I motioned for him to roll down the window. He acted as if it hadn't occurred to him to do so until I asked, but then cranked it down to see what I wanted.

"Hey, Ken, ready to switch drivers for a while?" I asked with more kindness than my panicked and impatient heart felt at the moment. He smiled sweetly and nodded. I looked over to the other sponsor riding in his car. She was sound asleep as well.

The teenagers in the backseat, however, were wide awake. They said they had been watching Ken swerve around for a mile or two, and it was hilarious. A couple of them had their driver's licenses and offered enthusiastically to take the wheel. It was tempting, but we had made the commitment before the trip that only adult sponsors would drive. So instead of letting one of the kids take control, we decided we'd spend a few minutes at the next rest stop pumping coffee into all the drivers and allowing the kids to fill up on soft drinks and junk food. Of course, that would only slow us down more in the bladder-filled miles that followed, but it seemed worth it to keep the whole caravan on the road.

While vehicle number three was switching drivers, I walked back to each of the other vehicles and assured them everything was all right. When I reached vehicle number four, the source of the shrieking report, I thanked Debbie for bringing the situation to my attention. Then I showed her how to adjust the volume control on her CB radio.

The Character Caravan

There's a sense in which, every day, our character travels around in these several different arenas, just like the vehicles on that youth trip. Within each vehicle are a couple of guys—the man in us and the boy in us—who take turns driving their arena. Usually when one drives, the other navigates. Together, they forge a mature

251

character trait that does well in that particular arena. And together, they're responsible for staying with the overall caravan and getting where they're going. But there's still only one caravan and one lead vehicle that's ultimately responsible for the trip.

That lead vehicle is analogous to the arena of perspective. In a sense, it's only one of several arenas, and there are several times on the interstate when another arena may even take the lead for a time. But the lead vehicle is still responsible for the whole caravan's direction, safety, and success.

Considering the fact that there are at least nine key character arenas, it may seem like we're giving undue importance to the perspective arena. After all, the arena of values is critical, relationships are eternally important, and one could even argue that the decision arena can change the whole character caravan as fast as any other.

But it's important to remember that the caravan of character arenas always moves together. When any other arena is allowed to lead the caravan, there are certainly going to be problems. In fact, when decisions or relationships or motives don't follow a wise perspective, it's a good sign that a brat or a jerk has found his way behind the steering wheel!

Some of the most tragic character tumbles we see today happen when the brat or jerk in someone jumps behind the wheel and an out-of-balance character trait from some other arena starts dictating to our overall perspective. For example, when our relationships don't flow out of a wise perspective, we might choose a destructive relationship because the "worthless jerk" in us has been made to feel special. When our work doesn't flow out of a wise perspective, we might grow lazy or dishonest on the job because the "perpetually bored brat" in us doesn't feel he's getting what he deserves. Even when the extremely important arena of values becomes the most important or "lead" arena to us, not having a God-centered perspective might lead us to embrace a social gospel, because the "nearsighted brat" would value helping people now more than helping people both eternally and now.

That's why, from the arena of perspective, we need to constantly check our side mirror and see if there's a problem in another character arena. Even though we're seeking to live from a God-centered perspective, we might notice that our priorities are shrieking, or that our discipline is swerving from side to side. That's when we have to pull the caravan over and bring wise perspective back to whatever arena is experiencing the problem. We have to ask ourselves, "Is that arena being ultimately controlled by a wise, God-centered perspective? If it is, we'll recognize that a balanced, Christ-like character trait is controlling the other arena as well.

There have been many times in my life when things seemed to be humming along tranquilly in the perspective arena. My faith in God was strong and I was generally seeking to follow His will. Then all of a sudden I'd find that something I said had hurt someone deeply. I'd run back to the communication arena and find that the tactful man in me had completely fallen asleep on the passenger's side, and that the unaccountable, truthful boy in me was about to wreck things. I needed to rouse the tactful man and let him drive for a while.

Meanwhile, in the backseat, the judgmental brat was chomping at the bit. "Don't bother bringing tact to this situation," I could hear him saying. "He's just as sleepy as truthfulness. Let ME drive for a while, and I'll tell this wimp with the hurt feelings about the wrong things HE's done . . ." Unfortunately, I've sometimes given in and let the brat drive. But hopefully the times are more and more frequent when I pour some coffee into my tact, ask sleepy truthfulness to navigate rather than drive for a while, and achieve a better balance of love in my communication arena.

I could give example after example of how wise perspective needs to occasionally run back and correct problems in the character caravan. But if the pages of this book have made sense, you can now do that too. It's really not all that complicated. All other arenas should all follow your core arena of God-centered perspective. The man in us and the boy in us should cooperate to bring a God-centered character trait to each arena. And even when the swerving starts, you never take the easy way out and let the brat or the jerk drive.

What to Pack and Who to Bring in the Lead Vehicle

To keep the whole character caravan together and moving forward happily can be a lot harder than moving sixty teenagers

253

across the country on a youth trip. Fortunately, we don't have to do it alone. Let's conclude by looking at the most important safety equipment and passengers to have along in the lead arena of our inner perspective—those who will keep wisdom in the driver's seat.

First, we need a good side mirror. By that I mean we need a genuine concern for our own maturity and character development. We need a willingness to monitor the kind of person we are and a desire to change for the best. It's when we're oblivious to the different character arenas of our life and how we're performing in each of them that wrecks are likely to happen.

Second, we need a good CB radio. Curves in the road and traffic on the highway can obscure the view between our character arenas. We need communication between the different arenas that allows us to recognize problems in one character trait from the vantage point of another. In making a responsible decision we may notice that we have a self-serving motive. By bringing greater focus to our priorities we may realize that our values have gotten out of whack. When a positive character trait is governing one arena, we can sometimes identify other arenas where the swerving has started.

Third, we need a good set of brakes. We need a willingness to stop and take corrective action. Hopefully it's been hammered into our heads by now that it takes both the boy in us and the man in us to develop positive, balanced character traits that will serve us well in each character arena. If the swerving does start, we need to switch drivers, to evaluate which part of our balanced driving team is dozing, and which part needs to have more influence. And if there's anything wise perspective can bring to that pulled-over arena, it's the recognition that brats and jerks are both selfish and should never be allowed to drive.

Fourth, we need women in the car with us. What? Isn't this male character thing sort of a macho, drum-beating exercise where we explore the male psyche and mine the depths of the distinctly male character? Well, you won't get very far into the male character before you discover a need for the female touch. Hopefully the many girls and women I've used in illustration have helped us recognize that. We need mothers, wives, daughters, sisters, and female friends. The women and girls in our lives help to both nurture the boy in us and soften the man in us. They can ride with us in the arena of perspective and give us another view. It's a point of view that is distinct from anything we could muster, and can give us an incredible, objective vantage point, if we'll turn the TV off and listen. The women in our lives who love us and want what's best for us are the best passengers we could hope for.

Fifth, and most important, we need God's own Holy Spirit. He is a gracious passenger, and as James 1:5 says, He's very willing to give wisdom to all who ask. I can't think back to the swerving car on that youth trip without realizing how perilously close to tragedy our whole caravan came. I can't imagine what it would have been like to face one of those kids' parents at the hospital, or the funeral home. God's great grace kept us safe on that dark highway, beyond what the mirrors or radios or brakes or passengers could ever do.

You see, God cares so very much for our little caravans, and for our character caravans as well. He knows our final destination. It's a destination where one day all our men and boys will pile out of our caravan and present the character traits they've learned along the journey. Then we'll see His own holy character. And we'll gratefully lay at His feet whatever God-centered character traits we've managed to put together on the way, for His glory.

Since you are God's dear children, you must try to be like him.
(Ephesians 5:1)